NEW AGE VS CHRISTIANITY

SEVEN HOUSE MEDIA

NEW AGE *VS* CHRIST- IANITY

THE HIDDEN DANGERS AND
DECEPTIONS OF SPIRITUAL HEALING

JOSCELYN A. BÁEZ
SABA TEKLE

SE7EN
HOUSE MEDIA

SEVEN
HOUSE MEDIA

Library of Congress Control Number: 2023932133
ISBN: 978-1-0880-9923-0
www.7housemedia.com
Copyright © 2022 Saba Tekle
Cover *7 House Media, LLC*
Editor *Kristina Beverlin*

All rights reserved. No part of this publication may be reproduced, distributed, or transmitted in any form or by any means, including photocopying, recording, or other electronic or mechanical methods, without the prior written permission of the publisher, except in the case of brief quotations embodied in critical reviews and certain other noncommercial uses permitted by copyright law. For permission requests, contact info@7housemedia.com.

Disclaimer:

Although the publisher and the author have made every effort to ensure that the information in this book was correct and while this publication is designed to provide accurate information in regard to the subject matter covered, the publisher and the author assume no responsibility for errors, inaccuracies, omissions, or any other inconsistencies herein and hereby disclaim any liability to any party for any loss, damage, or disruption caused by errors or omissions, whether such errors or omissions result from negligence, accident, or any other cause.

This publication is meant as a source of valuable information for the reader, however it is not meant as a substitute for direct professional assistance, such as a mental health professional. If such level of assistance is required, the services of a competent professional should be sought.

This work depicts actual events in the life of the author as truthfully as recollection permits. While all persons within are actual individuals, names and identifying characteristics have been changed to respect their privacy.

Dedicated to The God of Abraham, The God of Isaac, and the God of Jacob

Contents

Preface *1*

1 Testimony New Age Cocaine *Joscelyn Báez* *3*
   The Book That Made God Even More Confusing 7
   Dancer To Stripper To Hypnosis and Med-Free 8
   New Age Cocaine and Spiritual Healing 12
   Sage, Crystals and Micro-dosing 15
   The Demonic Storm 18
   The Aftermath 29
   I Was Lost, Found, Then Lost Again 31
   False Hindu God and Bad Luck 33
   Chakras and Ceremonies 36
   Deliverance 37
   Sin "Made" Me Do It 38
   A Fight With The Devil 42
   The Call of Christ 44

2 Testimony Unconscious Covenants *Saba Tekle*...*49*
   Introduction to Christianity 51
   Turning Point 52
   New Age, Family Drama, and Trauma 54
   Nothing But New Age and The Downsides 57
   Distaste and No Success 59
   Work Success and The Downfalls 60
   Healing 61

Spiritual Awakening a.k.a. Demonic Attack 63
The Biggest Turning Point 67
OH TULUM 69
My Exit Out Of New Age 72
My CC – Jesus and Jesus Alone 76
Saved by Grace 76
Holy Spirit 78
Unconscious Covenant With The Devil............ 81
A Message From God................................. 82
The Fight To Be Christian Continues.............. 88

3 New Age VS Christianity *Joscelyn and Saba*......*95*

History... 98
Who brought the New Age here 102
Babylon..104
In Closing...114

About The Author

References

Acknowledgements

Thank you Mom, Rita, and Casey for interceding for my salvation and deliverance. – *Joscelyn*

Thank you, Aster, my sister, for showing me by example what living in obedience to God looks like. - *Saba*

Ephesians 6:12
New King James Version

For we do not wrestle against flesh and blood, but against principalities, against powers, against the rulers of the darkness of this age, against spiritual hosts of wickedness in the heavenly places.

Preface

In this book, you are going to first read our testimonies, specifically the turning points in our lives that lead us from Jesus and back to Jesus. It includes how we were both demonically attacked. There were times when it was not as obvious and others when it was undeniable. This way you can detect and understand why you should navigate away from practices culturally infused with the New Age.

We share our raw and explicit stories in hopes that we can relate to your life and your walk with Christ. For those of you who are not Christian, we hope this plants a seed that will lead you to get saved. For others that are saved, our hope is to instill your faith, to strengthen your walk, and to help you see why spiritual practices outside of the Bible are dangerous and why God is protecting you from them.

Please understand that our stories begin with childhood and we cannot fit our entire story in the pages that follow. We broke our stories into pieces that are easy to digest and which lead straight to the turning points that led us astray and then back into His loving arms.

This book is meant for you to see how we learned that we need nothing but Jesus and anything outside of that, (i.e. the New Age) has the antichrist's spirit.

The New Age vs Christianity debate, where we break down each practice, begins at the end of our testimonies. The New Age presents itself as something which can accompany Christianity, but, in fact, it is demonic and rooted in Satanism. We learned this the hard way, and we are sharing what we learned with you so that you won't have to experience the same traumas and hardships that we did.

1
Testimony

New Age Cocaine
Joscelyn Báez

I had not slept all night. I lay trembling in terror on the couch. The only sound that filled the room was the deep breathing of my roommate as she slept. I looked up straining in the dark, trying to focus on one area on the ceiling, but the more I focused, the more I saw multiple lights and shapes contort into numerous complex patterns. It was like an over-stimulating video game. Every second I begged for it to stop but was unable to talk because I could hardly feel my own body. Just when I passed one level, the next level would begin. Each level was a new strata of seeming nightmares filled with demons that were impossible to beat. But this was not a nightmare, this was an LSD overdose on tabs created by a Shaman who practiced white and black magic…

My Beginning in the New Age...

My first experience with New Age was when I was about 8 years old in Columbus, Ohio. I walked past a New Age/Wiccan crystal shop and I felt a cold chill, like tiny fingers running up my arm and an uncomfortable fear. I had no idea what the store was, nor did I understand the products. Years later, I learned about my astrological sign (Gemini) when I became particularly interested in personality tests. That was the beginning of my interest in self-discovery, which soon led to a real encounter with the spirits behind those chilling, tiny fingers I had felt but had long forgotten about from my childhood.

My life had been full of various disasters – I was in an abusive relationship for 6 years that led to a suicide attempt, and I had been hospitalized in a mental ward twice. This resulted in strange episodes that led to a diagnosis of manic bipolar with psychotic symptoms.

My parents had divorced when I was in high school and the church they were pastoring had been dispersed. I generally avoided church after that. Before and after my hospitalizations, I had started working in nightclubs as a gogo dancer, which led to me becoming a stripper in 2 different clubs in Columbus. Initially, I did this to make extra money on the side while I was in college, especially since I was financially supporting my abusive boyfriend at the time. However, working in nightclubs is a hypnotic world. Once you get sucked in by the trance of easy money, free alcohol, and an escape from your problems, it is difficult to get out.

I moved to Los Angeles in November 2018 to pursue a career in professional dance. At least that is the reason I gave to people. The other reason was because in 2017, I had sat in my Corolla late at night and yelled at God to give me answers. This ended in a vision from God that would change my life forever. I was desperate to understand this vision and to figure out the purpose of my life, and I knew I had to get out of Ohio.

I moved in with a girl named Abby, who told me she was spiritual and kept energy-healing crystals around the apartment. Though I told her I did not mind, I thought to myself that it sounded rather stupid. Little did I know, I would soon be engulfed in New Age spirituality myself, and would experience what spiritualists call an "Awakening".

Within a year, I would experience the full brutality of Hollywood. I was molested by a famous actor. I was offered a deal to sell myself to a major rapper. I made money working as an underground nightlife karaoke hostess and a stripper, and I interned under a prominent music producer who propositioned me with sexual favors.

I felt more and more confused about who God really was, and why I had been abused my whole life. Hollywood is like a vortex which spirals so fast that you no longer have a true perception of time. One year can feel like three years and one month at the same time. The vortex is so disorienting that it will change who you are at an impossibly rapid rate while also leaving you wondering how it even happened in the first place.

It is a sinister, spiritual phenomenon that cannot be understood unless you experience it for yourself. Everything in my life and career was happening so fast that it was becoming a blur. I was extremely disappointed. I had finally made it to the city that I had daydreamed about since I was young, but everything I had worked for since I was a little girl was completely vain. The life that I had fought for was abusing me and proved time and time again that this lifestyle was a lie. But I was not ready to give up that lie, so I let the vortex take me deeper and deeper.

My roommate Abby added to my confusion. She knew that I grew up a Christian and was constantly preaching to me about New Age spirituality. I would ignore her, although I became desensitized to her practices which included psychedelic usage, shaman rituals, and snorting an Amazonian drug called Hapé.

The Book That Made God Even More Confusing

I was always the kind of woman that could not stick to just one "thing" – one venture, one skill, one interest, one job, one talent. Besides being a professional dancer, I was also a public speaker while in Ohio and had received an award for being an "Ambassador of Peace" by the Universal Peace Federation.

The Universal Peace Federation (UPF) is a sector of the United Nations that includes thousands of religious leaders, politicians, and activists from around the world. Their aim is to bring world peace and unity. I went to a UPF conference in Los Angeles, hoping I could pick up where I left off in Ohio and continue activism and public speaking in California. I met the director of the Los Angeles sector and we exchanged contact information. Before long, he scheduled to meet me for dinner. Over dinner, he shared with me the story of his spiritual awakening in his homeland, Iraq, and how he fled to the United States.

After dinner, he invited me to the UPF Los Angeles headquarters. It was a building on a hill with old-fashioned European architecture. He took me inside to the library and pulled out a book called *The Divine Principle*. He said, "Here. Read this. This book was written by our founder, Reverend Moon. A lot of the Christians in our organization don't like it, but you need an open mind to read this book, which you have. When you're done with it, I'll give you the next level of the book."

He told me how this book could not be found in any store or library — it is only distributed between their leaders. I later discovered that the book could be found online, but only the generalized versions. The book that was given to me by the director was a much more detailed version, about the revelation Reverend Moon received in the mountains in Korea, where he was seeking wisdom and truth from God. I was excited to read it, especially since it was not open to the public. It was hidden knowledge, something only the elite could have. The more I read the book, the more confused and doubtful I began to feel about the God of the Bible.

I had had many questions for God throughout my life, but never more so than in that moment. Who is God really? If He loves us, why does He only give us breadcrumbs of communication? If Jesus is the only way, why are there so many other gods like him? If God loves me so much, why have I been abused my whole life? How could there be hell?

From Dancer To Stripper To Hypnosis and Med-Free

Finding a sustainable job is very difficult in Los Angeles unless you have connections. I had difficulty finding work despite my degree and experience. I was running out of the little money that I had saved to move to Los Angeles when I saw an ad on Craigslist for a karaoke hostess.

It seemed shady, but I was both desperate and adventurous and I decided to give it a try. I worked as the "hostess" for only two months, an extremely taxing and dangerous job. It involved being driven around Koreatown in a minivan to multiple karaoke clubs to show myself off to the men in the reserved rooms and see if they wanted to rent me for entertainment for a couple of hours.

Naturally, these men usually expected me to be at least a little promiscuous, even if I was not willing to have sex in the room. Mafias would rent me and there would be so much coke passed around and spread on the tables. They would keep me longer if I let them carry out sexual acts on me, to the point of giving me marks, cuts, and bruises on my breasts and I would wake up the next day in pain. One night, I was drugged and had to be carried convulsing out of the club by my boss. I did not like the idea of being a stripper again, but ultimately decided to go back to it.

The strip club scene had been dying in Los Angeles because of new tax enforcement on strippers and yet the competition was still very high. If a girl was willing to engage in any form of sexual activity with a man in a VIP dance room, she would make much more money than a girl who would simply dance. There were times I had to fight men in VIP rooms because they were drunk and not satisfied with my physical boundaries. One man even followed me to my car and molested me with a dollar bill in the parking lot.

I had become increasingly desensitized to sex work, so letting men molest me in a VIP room was no longer difficult to accept. I would cry and feel disgusted and disoriented by how I hated the act but experienced my body still uncontrollably getting aroused by it. Then I would go back to work. I drank my despair away so I could stay in character for men's fantasies. Many times, however, I would leave the room sick to my stomach and running to the bathroom thinking I was going to puke. Some of these men would tell me that they did not know how to describe it, but that I had "healed" them through my touch and dance. The longer I stayed in sex work, the more I could feel demons on these men, my clients. With certain men, after I would dance on them, I would have flashes of imagery and an inner knowing that they had extreme sexual perversions, such as incest. I would often wake up feeling sick the next day. I experienced more and more sexual nightmares. Although this work was suffocating me, I had a day job as well, and I balanced both, along with my dance training and music video gigs.

With multiple jobs, I had more than enough money to pamper myself. I decided to go to Malibu for three days for my birthday in 2019, and I stayed in an Airbnb in the Topanga Canyon. I asked God to help me find my purpose as I thought about that vision I had in my car and my deep longing to dance and make music. On the second day of my trip, I ran into a man who was a hypnosis therapist. He invited me to an event and I attended my first hypnosis group session on my last night in Malibu. It felt so intoxicatingly powerful. We did an activity that involved a partner. I was paired up with a little boy and a few minutes into the session, I was uncontrollably crying. I felt like this boy was healing me. I sensed this boy had so many spiritual gifts and I could "see" so much in him. Everyone else's experience seemed normal and not so intense. Shortly thereafter, I quit stripping. For about a year, I continued hypnosis, and eventually started paying for private hypnosis sessions.

I weaned myself off the antipsychotic medication (Seroquel) that I had been taking ever since my second mental hospitalization, much to the dismay of my psychiatrist. My psychiatrist was greatly opposed but was reassured when I told her I would use holistic practices to help in the process. I was determined to be completely medication-free, although I was told that manic bipolar was incurable. I was having more visions and dreams and was becoming desperate for spiritual answers to life and who I really was. I was seeing "angel numbers" (repetitive numbers in sequence i.e., 4444, 3333) constantly.

There were times when I would wake up and see flashes of light above me or forms fighting on the ceiling. Somehow, I knew there was a battle going on over my life. I met a woman who told me when she would see me that she would have visions of a peacock. That was fascinating to me because my dad got a tattoo of a peacock with my name written on it to represent me when I was born. I did some research based on my racial heritage being Puerto Rican, and discovered that a peacock is an "incarnation" of the Puerto Rican goddess, Oshun. "Daughters of Oshun" are Puerto Rican women who usually have dancing talent, beauty, and psychic abilities. It made me wonder. That woman seemed to read me. She told me to "let the messages out" from my visions and dreams and that I should no longer hold them in. It seemed like all the dots were connecting without me even trying.

New Age Cocaine and Spiritual Healing

My interest in New Age holistic healing deepened as I continued my hypnosis sessions. I was having sexual nightmares that deeply disturbed Abby, who recognized how all of this was impacting me.

Abby had heard my stories of how my clients in strip clubs would tell me how my touch and dances would heal them, and how I could sense specific demonic presences on them to the point that I would feel sick. She knew the darkness of being a karaoke hostess and a stripper was still haunting me, along with the sexual harassment and abuse I faced in the industry, so she recommended I go with her to a Yoni ceremony. The purpose was to spiritually cleanse your sexual and reproductive organs.

I went with her to the venue. Both of us wore long skirts and prepared bowls for the cleansing steam. Abby's shaman prepared the herbs and water and we each took some in our bowls. Every woman sat in a circle, and we prepared to hover over the bowls and let the steam enter our privates, cleansing us from all physical, sexual, and spiritual impurities and traumas. Before we proceeded, the shaman and her apprentice gave each of us Hapé. It was my first time taking it and I was nervous. It never sat right with me, seeing my roommate take this wooden tube, quickly blow this gray powder up her nose, and lean back, breathing deeply and sighing like she had just gotten a deep dose of New Age cocaine.

I would see her snort it several times a day, and she took it with her everywhere she went. Abby kept telling me how it would align my chakras and help ground me, so I finally decided to give it a try. That shaman sat across from me cross-legged, staring deeply into my eyes, and told me to take a long breath and hold it in.

As I held my breath, she blew in the Hapé through one end of the tube and it shot up my nostril where the other side of the tube was. I retained my breath for a few more seconds, then released it through my mouth. When I released my breath, tears immediately rolled down my cheeks and I felt this exhilarating energy surge through my body as a burning sensation filled my nose. My body felt intensely high but deeply connected to the floor and to everyone around me at the same time. I laid back and was suddenly filled with memories of pedophiles who had preyed on me when I was little. I could see their faces and remember the fear and insecurity I felt. I wept and felt myself releasing the memories with each passing second.

At the end of the session, the shaman did a tarot card reading on me. She interpreted the card I picked, saying that all my dreams will come true and that I can manifest them. This affirmation of all that I had been striving for gave me all the pleasant, ooey-gooey feelings inside that I always wanted.

That was my only time attending a Yoni ceremony, but my interest in New Age spirituality continued to increase. As the months went along, however, I would still have more and more visions and random "messages" about people, and especially about world events. Amid those messages, I would also get random visions that would make me scream and cry, and I did not know what the meaning of these visions was. One instance of this was when I had a vision of seeing a baby's fingers getting chopped off. I had no control of when a vision would happen.

Sometimes the visions would come in a trance, but sometimes I would receive imagery that was very vivid and intrusive. There were nights I would wake up in emotional torment and see that something terrible was going to happen to the world and millions of people would die. Uncontrollable words and predictions would fly out of my mouth. I saw that a man would die and would be considered a sacrifice and that people all over the world would mourn him. Little did I know, these messages were about Covid and the death of George Floyd.

Sage, Crystals and Micro-dosing

One night in the winter of 2020, I was in an Uber, and I found myself talking to the driver about my life and my pursuits and successes in the industry. This was uncommon because I never engaged in long conversations in Ubers. I even told him about my experience with the UPF and how I cut off the director when he clearly had romantic interests in me. I told him that with every month that passed, the more I wondered if anything at all was real.

He said, "Well, do you really want to know?" My interest peaked and I said, "Yes! I do!" He said, "Okay, I'm going to give you some names of people to look up on your own and I'll give you my phone number so you can contact me if you have any questions. Be ready. Everything you've known is a lie. I know you said you grew up a Christian but just keep an open mind. You're already part of the way there, but this didn't happen for no reason. You were supposed to be in this car right now. You're ready for this."

He listed some names like David Icke and The Real Merkabah, and I eagerly wrote them in the notes app on my phone. As soon as I got home, I thanked him and started on my research. Meanwhile, I had progressively weaned off my antipsychotic medication down to the last set of milligrams.

Abby was pleased with my gradual acceptance of the New Age, so she started giving me books to borrow, as well as sage, palo santo, and crystals. She would give me bracelets and necklaces with crystals on them for protection. She started grinding up shrooms into powder and putting them into capsules for me to take micro-doses to go deeper into the holistic healing process for my mind. I took 1-2 capsules every other day, and I did not notice a huge difference, but generally, I was more peaceful.

A few weeks after my first micro-dose, I went on a shroom trip with Abby. I started off with a light dosage for the trip. Abby said she would not even get any hallucinatory visuals with that small of a dose, but for me, I saw and felt so much. I looked at my arm and could see the hairs growing and moving with vibrant life, like watching seaweed dance in a reef. When I looked at the houseplants, I saw them moving and breathing with aura colors. When I reached out to them, they would reach back out to me.

I felt so alive and filled with supernatural power, and yet so powerless to the drug and to the universe around me. I loved how I could see everything, such as the rug or a pillow, morph into different designs and I could see even the threads of the fabric like I was looking through a microscope. My mind and eyes would create breathtaking designs within those designs and within those still. There were endless possibilities, and I could create them without limitation when I was on shrooms, because my vision was amplified by what seemed like a magnitude of hundreds. It was so spectacular to me, especially since I had been wearing glasses since I was about 7 years old, and my natural eyesight was very limited.

The trip confirmed what I had been feeling for years – that I had potent spiritual gifts, and even more than that, some type of spiritual power that made me so different from other people. I was never normal, and I never would be. But I also began to feel and believe other things – that I was not really here, and that I was more spiritual than everyone else. My body was here, but my soul and spirit were not. I felt like I was learning so much more about God than I ever learned in church. I concluded that one must learn about God within oneself.

The Demonic Storm

It all led up to that fateful night – my first night completely weaned off Seroquel. I had experienced a few withdrawal symptoms throughout the process, but nothing too drastic. I felt a little nervous as I laid down to sleep, but I was also so excited because this was the moment I had been waiting for. I would now be free. I knew whatever spiritual power was being suppressed in me all these years that was partially numbed with medication would be freed and I could reach my true potential. I felt like an alien, and I was ready to dive deeper into my mind and God.

That night, I did not sleep at all. I tossed and turned, and as the hours progressed, I began to sweat profusely. My heart was pounding. Then my mind was flooded with vivid memories that I had forgotten about for years. Random pictures filled my mind – trees, dresses, cups, faces. It was like the gears that had been stopped for years were now turning at top speed, and I felt the edge of insanity. The only thing that helped me get through was playing New-Age frequency music and gripping my Bible in my arms as I laid in bed, quivering.

Everything I predicted about how I would be when I was completely Seroquel-free came true. I could not sleep all the way through the night. The days that followed were filled with visions. I would wake up and go to the bathtub and sit in it, crying while psychic messages would flood my mind. I had always felt people's emotions and their personal struggles just from being around them, talking to them, or touching them, which is one of the reasons I liked to spend a lot of time alone. Now that I was off medication, that ability increased exponentially.

I kept myself locked away in my bedroom as much as possible. I could feel the energy of plants and being around them made me feel much more grounded. My sense of sound seemed to heighten, and certain sounds became unbearable to me, especially machinery. I had a much lower alcohol tolerance.

When Abby would bring friends over, I would sense certain demonic presences on them or specific issues, and then the person would end up talking about it and confirming what I sensed. If someone entered the vicinity with intense depression, I would sense it immediately and feel myself on the brink of tears. But it was not just a feeling – I would have visions of their torment and feel it as vastly and powerfully as they did — like it was happening directly to me. If I felt someone was dabbling in black magic, I would be accurate, and I would feel sick to my stomach. I thought these were just the gifts God gave me. But it was beginning to feel more like an infectious curse that was stronger than I could handle.

May was my birthday month. A few weeks leading up to it, I heard a voice say that May would be an important month for me, and that I would have a huge awakening – that the kingdom would be given to me. I thought it was the Kingdom of God that Jesus spoke about, and I thought it was God speaking to me. It felt so intense that it stirred up both anxiety and excitement in me at the same time.

Then, about two weeks before May, Abby asked me if I would go on an LSD (acid) trip with her and her friend. She had gotten tabs of LSD from her shaman who made it herself. I had a gut feeling telling me not to do it, but she kept telling me how it would be almost exactly like shrooms, except not as strong. She told me the imagery on acid is more like being in a computer, with technological types of shapes and patterns. She also said it would really help heal my mind and cleanse it from the years of antipsychotic meds and that it would strengthen my spiritual abilities.

A few nights before the acid trip, I had more trouble sleeping than usual. I kept "hearing" a voice saying "I'm calling YOU", and I thought it was God. It seemed to contradict the encouraging voice I heard before that told me May would be a powerful month for me, and I did not really know what it meant. It was like the voice was trying to tell me that I already knew what was right and wrong and to stop and listen. But I could not. My mind was filled with racing thoughts, and I was so tired from lack of sleep. So my very first LSD trip was scheduled for May 2, 2020.

My experience on acid was something that I will not ever be able to fully explain. Abby convinced me to take two tabs instead of one because she and her friend were taking that amount as well. Just like what we did before taking shrooms, we sat in a circle and set our intentions and said a prayer to the universe (I prayed to God). Then we took the tabs together, placing the thin, dark brown film on our tongues and let it melt. I did not start to feel deep in the trip until about 40 minutes in. Just like with shrooms, as my mind began to fall into this altered state of consciousness, I had this revelation that my soul had been picked up and thrown into a field in the universe.

I had absolutely no control over what could happen. I was unprotected and uncovered, with the natural veil that stops our minds from thinking every thought possible being ripped off my consciousness. With shrooms, I at least felt rooted and one with the earth. With this, I felt that I was in the realm of "Anything" – deep into the tree of the knowledge of good and evil. Nobody, not even my own will and thoughts, could stop this drug from taking me wherever it wanted. It was scary, but I could not even physically or emotionally react because I could not move on the sofa.

Psychedelics made my senses so extremely heightened, but at the price of my body feeling so heavy I could not move. I would sit or lay in one position for what felt like hours, and it would be sometimes impossible to stand or walk entirely. In the first two hours, we had so much fun. Abby and I were rolling on the floor laughing to the point of tears, and I had found an ant crawling on the couch, picked it up, and given it a name. I could see all parts of the ant so microscopically, just like when I had tripped on shrooms.

About an hour after that, Abby's friend felt like she needed to work through some past sexual traumas and wanted to take some Hapé. She sat cross-legged on her living room floor and snorted the powder. She went into a trance and I began to feel uncomfortable for some reason, so I stood up, watching her as I leaned against her kitchen counters. In her trance, she began rocking back and forth and making a sound with her mouth. I cannot remember the sound anymore, but I do remember it sounded so morbid and demonic, it made me run out of the apartment. I had a vision of light beaming into her body from the ceiling and then shooting out horizontally as she was in this trance. But it was not a good light. I did not understand how a white light could actually be so evil. The sound she was making was something I have never heard before, and yet it seemed like every part of my inner being recognized the sound. Somehow, I knew it was a demonic language. The whole room filled with the presence of something so evil that I had to get away as soon as possible. The presence was so ferocious, consuming, and wicked, I felt that if I stayed there a second longer, I would get pulled into utter darkness. The light was bright, and yet it was a black hole.

It was the devil. I kept thinking, "The devil himself has entered." I had never been somewhere where I had felt something so evil that merely the feeling of it on my skin was enough to make me beg for death. I did not know evil could be that strong.

Most people could never imagine what it is like to see or feel something so depraved that your entire body, heart, and soul are begging to die just so you can stop seeing, hearing, or feeling it. This is what being completely devoid of God is like. Even if you live a corrupt life, it is not the same as being surrounded by an atmosphere that itself is completely devoid of God. But in that moment, I entered into a world that encompassed that level of God-less deprivation. I couldn't feel the breeze, the joy from seeing beautiful flowers, or the peace from hearing birds sing. It was like God's own breath and mark of His handiwork was removed from everything around me. And nobody could see it but me.

I ran outside and sat in the grass, looking out at the trees before me. There was a fountain to my left, and a couple feet beyond that was the beach. The fear was unlike anything I had ever experienced before. I had experienced deep pits of gut-wrenching fear when I had been sexually abused, while being locked in rooms and restrained by my ex-boyfriend, and when standing over a bridge when I was contemplating suicide. And yet, those fears seemed like a pebble, and this fear was a mountain. I felt stuck in the worst nightmare possible, and yet there was no way out. My heart pounded and I desperately took deep breaths in through my nose and out through my mouth, trying to stop a panic attack.

And that is when it happened.

The demon that had taken over my roommate's friend had followed me from the apartment. She was still stuck in the trance with her eyelids fluttering and rocking back and forth. That demon entered my mind, and I remember the exact moment it did so. I could literally feel a being inside of me under my skin. I aggressively began scratching at my skin because the being felt so dirty. The thing itself was complete chaos. It was filled with hatred, and it knew me — HE knew me. It felt like a man. I had no idea how I knew these things; I just did. He started speaking to me and showing me what he saw in his perverted mind. These were all things I was incapable of thinking in my own mind, and never had seen or heard in my life. My own mind seemed to be locked in a cage, screaming in terror, frantically trying to stay in control of my will, emotions, and my body. Then, that's when it got worse, far beyond what I thought was even possible.

He told me to strip naked and masturbate in front of the children outside. Terror, disgust, and complete anguish filled my heart. Tears streamed down my face. I could not believe this was happening. I had never heard a voice like that before. I did not desire to do anything even remotely close to that, nor have I ever in my entire life. The movement underneath my skin and this horrendous voice that had entered my mind was completely against my will, and each passing second caused me to spin into a whirlwind of insanity. He showed me that everyone and everything was sexual, and he showed me what his imagination was like — that anything sexual was possible.

It suddenly hit me: the knowledge in the New Age was infinite, but Abby, her friend, and I were no better than the crackheads we saw roaming the streets of Los Angeles — harnessing the need to be in an altered state of reality. I suddenly understood what the mind of someone on meth or heroin was like, and how their soul was wandering and they could not get it back. They were stuck in this black hole that I had entered. I was quickly spiraling deeper and deeper still.

He began to threaten me. He wanted me to completely obey him in every way, and he was furious at me. Everything around me seemed to spin. I fell into a complete panic because I felt that this was not real — the trip was not real, the world itself was not real, and I was not real. Looking around me was unnerving. I felt like I was in a video game and nobody else realized they were in one, and that I had to escape or else the torture would increase. The only way to escape was suicide.

I looked down at the grass because sitting on the ground and burying my toes in the grass always made me feel more peaceful. But now, even the grass terrified me. I grabbed it and hysterically pulled the strands up out of the ground. I looked up and saw that parents who were outside playing with their kids were staring at me, pulling their kids close to them. Some were taking their kids back inside. I had frightened the children, and the thought alone broke my heart. I looked back down at the grass, and the demon began telling me and showing me in my mind what hell is really like. I was so deep in this altered state of reality. This being had dragged me through a door into another state of consciousness where the revelation of demons resides.

He showed me that hell was an endless time loop of your deepest, darkest fear over and over, done in a creative way that only demons can form in their own imagination. For me, the desire for suicide that was buried in my past had resurfaced, and I knew that if there was a gun next to me, I would pick it up and shoot myself in the head without a second thought. But then, I would wake up, just to experience the same agonizing thoughts and demonic revelations that would quickly send me into suicide again and again and again.

I screamed for Abby. She ran outside and sat next to me and asked what was wrong. I cried, "The devil is here. It came onto her. And it followed me outside. I want to kill myself." She told me to calm down and follow her inside. She put her arm around me and guided me back into the apartment because I could still hardly stand up properly. Her friend asked what was wrong when she saw me trembling and crying. She said she had no idea what had happened when she went into that trance. She said all she saw was what looked like disco lights.

The rest of the night was a complete terror. Every second felt like an hour. I felt like I was in a timeless void of anguish and darkness. Abby told me to take Hapé to realign my chakras, so I did, and it calmed me down somewhat — just for a moment. I was still shaking, so Abby took me into her friend's bed and tried to get me to compose myself, but I could not stop shaking. I could still feel something underneath my skin, inside of me, crawling, whispering, thinking in my brain while shoving my own mind into a cage. I could not describe to Abby what was happening because the psychedelics made it difficult for me to talk.

Also, how do I tell someone that someone else had entered into my mind and was telling me knowledge and revelations of evil? I wanted to stare at something plain like the wall, because if I looked at anything or anyone else, this thing would show me their sexuality, and how everything and everyone was sexual. It was completely out of my character. I had been overtaken by something — or someone — else.

The Aftermath

I threw up 4 times that night. Each time, it was a black liquid with what appeared to be blood in it. Abby's friend said she felt a strange anger towards me and did not know why because she never felt animosity towards me before. When she looked at me, I saw the demon who I knew had chased me outside. Her face became dark, old, and masculine. As soon as she turned and I saw that demon, I ran into the bathroom to puke. It looked so evil that it made me nauseous. I silently asked for Jesus to help me. I felt ashamed to even ask Him to help me because I was not even sure if He existed at this point, and if He did, why would He want to help ME?

I thought, how could He want to help me, if He IS real? I had been avoiding Christianity for so long.

Later that evening, I laid on the couch in the living room. My roommate slept a few feet away from me on some pillows to keep an eye on me since I had talked about wanting to kill myself earlier. I laid there, staring into the distance, and still seeing all the endless patterns morphing into other new patterns, still shaking.

And that was when I saw him. A man in all white was walking towards me. It was a compelling vision, so I was seeing this unfold like it was a dream. As he walked closer, I thought to myself, "This must be Jesus." It had to be. He was so pure and filled with a clean light — not like the light I saw on Abby's friend. Looking back now, I believe it was an angel of the Lord. He came and knelt before me to stare directly into my eyes. He was so holy and unlike any man I had ever seen. I stared back in complete awe and almost fear as well. He did not say a word to me, but his authoritative eyes said it all:

"You know better. You shouldn't be here."

A young woman I knew was holding me in her arms in the vision. He turned to her and said, "Stay here with her. I have to tend to the rest."

Then I looked to my right. There were hundreds of people, each curled up into a ball, shaking and sobbing like me. They all were on drugs — they all had overdosed. That is exactly what this was. I had overdosed on LSD. For the next few minutes, I started preaching. I do not remember everything I said. The only thing I remember saying is:

"This is why we need Jesus. God is so holy, we need someone to be the bridge to God. Jesus is the bridge to God."

I did not come back until 28 hours later — the very next day. All night and all the following day until I came down from my high, my whole body was shaking. The entire night I hadn't slept. I honestly thought I would never come back psychologically. I wondered if I would have to be in the mental hospital the rest of my life, because it seemed impossible to come back to a normal state of consciousness. That is how deep in the black hole I was. Even though I did come back, something was wrong.

I took a shower the next day and as I stood under the warm water, that being who had entered my body during the LSD trip suddenly spoke again in my mind. It said, "Stay under the water." It wanted me to drown myself. I silently kept washing my hair and ignored the voice. It was not as loud as when I was on the LSD trip. I just wanted to forget it all, but I knew I would not. I knew I would never be the same after that. I had faced the devil and came out on the other side with a new level of spirituality — and a new level of horror stuck in my soul which was unutterable. I could not even express the being I felt, saw, and heard. Even uttering its words was too atrocious and evil to bear or hear.

I Was Lost, Found, Then Lost Again

Still, even with the vision I had on LSD, I could not let go of the New Age. It seemed to make too much sense, even though one question led to another — and another — and another. New Age spirituality was like the rabbit hole of knowledge that made me feel dominant, smart, and hungry for more all at the same time. It gave me a sense of peace, and yet I would feel uncomfortable with how open-ended and subjective every concept was. I continued reading New Age books to keep diving into the philosophy of this spirituality and the universe. The philosophy felt wise and profound, yet not entirely satisfactory. I had to keep digging for more revelations and more knowledge.

In the months that followed, I still was experiencing the intense clairvoyance and empath abilities that would drive me to depression and anxiety. The visions persisted, and many of them were about what seemed to be the end of the world and natural disasters. If I had a vision or a sense of a specific disaster happening somewhere in the world, I would google it to see if it was happening currently, and it would be.

Abby invited me to her shaman's house where she took bufo for the first time. Bufo is another shamanistic drug like ayahuasca that is highly concentrated DMT from the venom of a desert toad, but it is specifically used to exorcise a person and cause spiritual ascension. This shaman's house was one of the most enthralling houses I had ever been in. It was filled with beautiful artwork, Native American relics, Bohemian-styled furniture and accessories, and statues from other religions. I sat in the backyard during the ceremony, and the shaman administered the drug. Within a matter of seconds, Abby laid on her back as the shaman's assistant beat on a drum louder and louder. Abby began to writhe on the floor and contort in a highly sensual, animalistic manner. Her eyes were like saucers, and she stared up at the sky, mouth gaping open.

I felt an intense energy around me and my heart started pounding. It was uncomfortable and so extraordinary that I could not sit still. I stood up and ran to the wooden fence in the back. I began to jump up and down and laugh loudly, but inside, I did not feel any joy — just overstimulation. I had no idea why I did that. I was sensitive to feeling spirits, and whatever this was, was so strong that it influenced me to do something entirely strange. I came back and sat down. Shaking, I watched as Abby took another dose and fell under the spell again. In the middle of it as she rolled around on the ground, she turned to me, frozen in a robotic smile, and said, "I love you." Her eyes were huge and unblinking, looking lifeless, as if she were no longer a human.

False Hindu God and Bad Luck

After the ceremony, Abby wanted to get a Hindu god statue of Ganesh that she had seen in the shaman's house. Ganesh was supposed to bring good luck, but after she brought it into the house and set it on her altar, nothing but bad situations began to happen. I lost my keys and checked in my purse several times. After several hours, I looked back in my purse, and they were in a pocket that I had already looked in. A part of Abby's car was stolen on two different occasions within days, and she also lost her keys. I had a nightmare about Ganesh, in which I was left shivering, curled up in a ball in front of the statue. I told Abby about the dream and how I felt all of these bad things were happening because of Ganesh, so she threw it out. After that, we no longer had any "bad luck" situations at the apartment.

However, I found that I could not stay in the apartment for long unless I was sleeping. I had such a high sensitivity to the spirit realm around me, and the ability to know what kind of demons people who were around me had increased. One of those people was Abby. I would have nightmares about the demons she carried and about the things she really thought about me. Even just stepping out of my room, I would feel cold chills and a sickness creep into my body. I was hardly eating. I would sit outside and practice grounding, taking off my shoes and sitting in the small patches of grass around the block. The feeling of being on the edge of insanity was lingering, watching me around every corner. Being by a tree would help sedate me somewhat but not enough. I would take deep breaths, trying to get my mind to focus on reality so that I would not drift into the feeling of not knowing what was real and what was not. I could feel demons outside in the air as well. I could not escape them.

My aunt from New York gave me some tips on how to get rid of evil spirits. Many people in my family practice Santeria and some, even Brujeria. One of the practices she recommended was sitting in a bath with flowers and showering with cold water. I did both but neither helped.

In August 2020, I moved into my own studio apartment. My first night there, I hardly had any belongings — just an air mattress with a beach towel as my blanket. But I had something money could not buy — tranquil solitude. I was so blissful laying there with that little beach towel. The nightmares subsided, and I thought that now I was safe. I was wrong.

I continued having premonitions, and one of them was that I would meet a man who would change my life and career. I met that man, and because of him, I had the best-paying job I ever had outside of stripping. Even with what seemed like a success, I was still tormented at home. I would still get extremely perverted nightmares, including ones of me being raped. They felt so real. I would wake up and wonder if it was real or not. I was very busy, so I would shove those thoughts to the back of my mind.

Chakras and Ceremonies

The nightmares increased whenever I was sexually inactive, as if something wanted me to continually have sex and would punish me if I did not. I continued reading my New Age books and began to follow meditation practices that were recommended. One of them described sitting in meditation and taking deep breaths, focusing on each chakra. Then, one would call all of their energy from their past back to them. The breaths into each chakra seemed to help, and I would see a pulsating purple or indigo color when I closed my eyes. When I called my energy back to me, I felt an overwhelmingly powerful presence start to fill the room and my body. I was still in the state of meditation with my eyes closed, then my breathing became faster and faster.

The energy was chilling and I felt like it would completely overtake me. I forced myself out of the meditation, which was dangerous to do. I was gasping for air. I looked at my hands, and my palms were pulsating with a dark purple hue. I placed my left hand on the wall and removed it. The purple hue stayed on the wall and did not disappear for several minutes. The power that I had been trying to uncover by weaning off medication was here, but it was slowly consuming me.

Deliverance

In the beginning of 2021, I finally hit my breaking point. I had a great paying job working on the beach everyday, was creating music, and calling the shots in every area of my life. But no matter how much I busied myself, the dreadful memories of the demons and the perverted nightmares would drag me into hysteria, to the point that I would curl up on my bathroom floor and try to stop myself from running outside, ripping my clothes off and screaming.

There was a woman I met when I first moved to Los Angeles when I was trying out different churches. She had kept in touch with me even when I would disappear for a while, calling to check on me and make sure I was okay. I called her to see if she knew anyone who did deliverances. I knew it existed in Christianity, although I did not know much about it. All I knew was that I was determined to feel normal, and have this demon — or demons — off of me and out of my life. The first deliverance I had was outside at a park. The woman who did my deliverance believed some things that I did not agree with, like that homosexuality and meditation were wrong. I did not care though. I just needed this thing out of me.

Most of what I remember from the deliverance involved me thrashing and rolling in the grass, screaming out while the woman held onto me and told different types of demons to leave. I was not in control of my body. The demonic manifestations were so strong that she scheduled a second deliverance with another woman there. These deliverances lasted hours, and the second one was more terrifying. Different voices were speaking through me. I tried to strip naked, cut myself with my nails, and choke myself. Afterwards, I went back to my regular life. I felt free.

I knew I was free. I was moving up at my job and making new friends in the industry. I had a premonition that my ex-lover, who was my neighbor when I lived in Koreatown, would re-enter my life, and he had. I told myself I could maintain boundaries with him, and that I had time to figure out what to really think about Jesus. Life was good. Actually, life was so good, I made one of the worst mistakes I ever made in my life. I started sleeping with my ex-lover again.

Sin "Made" Me Do It

Juan and I were addicted to each other. Although I said I would never get into a non-committed sexual relationship again, I did with him. I knew about his gang history, his addiction to alcohol and lean, and that he would sleep with other women from time to time. It was a toxic situation. I would get premonitions of him — like the premonition I had that he would re-enter my life. He called me a psychic. I went right back to him, although I had a bad, sinking feeling.

This one mistake brought back all the demons I had before, with new ones. It did not happen immediately, so I thought I was safe and kept sleeping with this man. But after a couple of weeks, the torture began. I was assaulted at my job and was in and out of the hospital for various random health reasons. I would have dreams of other people's sexual secrets and I would wake up screaming in horror. This whole time after my first deliverance, I wrestled more between Christianity and the New Age. There still was so much in Christianity that did not make sense, and yet the New Age did not have the answers. It was just circles within circles of subjective truth, filled with the promises of freedom through shamans and drugs that cost thousands of dollars. Jesus was free, but did not make sense to me.

After some nights of prayer, I would suddenly get revelations of who God really is. With these revelations, a soft wave of peace would wash over me. I would write out everything. I would suddenly gain understanding — like how there has to be an absolute truth unlike what the New Age was teaching me, otherwise we would not even exist. Love cannot be whatever we make it to be because love must be an absolute truth, which is the definition of order and boundaries. Absolute truth has boundaries, a single definition.

It is this type of love that keeps the veil over our minds — the same veil that was ripped off of me when I took acid and no longer was protected from every form of knowledge that existed in the spiritual world. I would weep and sit in silence on my bed, feeling like there was a light in the distance that I was walking towards — a clean light. On one of those nights, I decided to write a covenant to Jesus Christ, even though I still did not understand everything about Him. I just knew He had to be the truth.

But this was when the real fight began. To describe everything that happened to me leading up to June would be impossible because I still cannot remember everything to this day. I did not write most of the things I experienced down in my journal because it was too evil to bear, and I do not want to ever read about it again.

However, there are things I can remember without looking at the journal entries I did write. I remember the day I woke up and saw my New Age tapestry that was hanging on my wall, suddenly hovering before my face. I had 20/20 vision which was impossible without my contacts in or glasses on. I would have nightmares of different demons trying to get me to sexually abuse other people. This psychic power would heighten in my dreams. I would have dreams of beings telling me about my abilities, and I would wake up after feeling the intense energy and that evil bright light starting to overtake me.

I had a dream with a celebrity giving me a spell to break a soul tie, and I did the spell when I woke up, thinking it was from God. I had more nightmares of witches and warlocks appearing to me, some trying to make me do the most atrocious things. Some gave me the darkest kinds of occult knowledge that I would wake up and bawl, wanting to forget everything. I would wake up feeling a body on top of me and hands wrapped around my head. This being would blow his breath into my third eye.

Sometimes I would walk downtown from work and feel the panic of not knowing whether I was in a dream or not, and this continued to grow until I found myself thinking of different ways to harm myself. I had no idea this was a thought disorder called depersonalization and derealization, and it was an extremely delusional form of agony that left my mind twisted. Simultaneously, I began losing my taste for alcohol and vulgar music.

Two weeks before my birthday in May, I had a premonition about the date June 10th, that this would be a life-changing event for me spiritually. When I had this premonition, I cried out to God on my bathroom floor and said, "Oh God! Kill all the old versions of me! I want them to die!"

Soon after, I walked out of my job without notice after being betrayed and used by the same person I had a premonition that I would meet. I was now unemployed and lost. The heartache was unbearable, and I was isolated in my apartment for days.

And this was when the devil visited me.

A Fight With The Devil

Around the first of June, I wept on my bed and asked God to take away all of my sexual desires. On June 2, I woke up, and my desires were completely gone — including my bisexual tendencies. It was utterly supernatural. As the days progressed, I realized that I could not even remember what sex felt like. But that thing in me that did not want me to stop having sex knew this and revealed itself. On June 3rd leading up to June 10th, I had a fight with the devil.

A demon was in my apartment and on June 10th, I could almost tangibly see him at one point. He was the same demon I had experienced when I overdosed on LSD. But this time, I was sober and I tried to fight back. He gave me visions from his own mind, showing me how he created scenarios of sexual torment. I screamed at him in my apartment and threw things. But each time I screamed at him in retaliation, he would stab me with another vision. I would fall to the ground and grab my head, screaming and crying.

It was still hard for me to say Jesus' name and my mind was a fog of complete darkness. The demon filled the air in my apartment, and it was thousands of times worse than being physically beaten. I told God I would rather be raped over and over and over than experience this, and I truly meant that. The vision attacks would be so morbid, I would sometimes lay on my floor naked, trembling in fear, feeling completely disconnected from my body. At this point, I began to think that the visions possibly occurred in real life in my past, and I no longer knew what was a true memory and what wasn't. I had lost my mind, and this time, it was for more than 28 hours.

I could hardly remember who I was or events from my past, because I did not even know what was a true or false memory anymore due to the visions and nightmares. I lost track of the days during this time period, because I felt that I was in an alternate state of reality. June 10th was when I completely broke. I could not feel my heart anymore. All of the love and compassion I felt for others had left. I did not even feel love for my family. I could hardly remember who they even were. My soul had died, and I could hardly even remember what it was like to create as an artist. It was a supernatural phenomenon that changed my life forever. This was my worst nightmare, and I had lost complete control. I knew that if I did not get help soon, the demon would find a way to kill me, or I would kill myself.

The Call of Christ

A few days later, I searched on Youtube for a salvation prayer video. I found one and knelt at my bed. After repeating the prayer narrated in the video and repenting for all of my sins, I closed my eyes as tears fell down my face. Then, the smell of beautiful flowers filled the apartment. I opened my eyes, stood up, and began walking around my apartment and even looking out my windows, checking to see if flowers were around. There were none. The smell was so beautiful, serene, and sweet. That is when I realized – the smell was Jesus. Jesus had walked into the room. There was nothing as pure as this.

I went through another deliverance with the same woman who did it months prior. I told her how I had sinned and had not fully given up New Age practices until now. This deliverance was much worse for me than the first time. My head felt like it was spinning, and I began behaving like a snake uncontrollably. Something screamed through me, and it penetrated the air so loudly both ears popped and I thought I had gone deaf. It was physically impossible for me to scream that loudly on my own. The very next day after that deliverance, I was suddenly healed from a physical affliction I had. It just disappeared.

I gave up my career in the industry because as soon as this shift began to happen with seeking Christ, my desire for Hollywood disintegrated. I lost my job, belongings, friends, heart, mind, and memories. Jesus was the only one who restored each of those lost pieces. Each piece came with a poem, His own distinct way of gently bringing back my mind from all of the fragmented pieces. After battling demons for weeks, my mind had begun to split and I was afraid to even step outside.

The depersonalization and derealization was so persistent, I would bang my head on the wall, and hit my own privates in agony, begging God to take away the memories of the demons tormenting me sexually, and the men who would take advantage of me in strip clubs and the karaoke clubs. But when I finally began calling His name, miracles began happening. If I would get attacked by a physical pain that was from a demon, I would scream out for Jesus, and He would enter the room. I experienced a holy peace that was so fulfilling that I did not have to keep digging for knowledge and ascension.

I moved back to my hometown in Ohio, where God took me through more deliverances. All of the demonic voices left, and every bipolar and PTSD symptom I once had never returned. I lost the desire to fulfill the dreams I had for most of my life with the industry, but that does not mean it was not difficult.

Being back in Ohio and starting all over again was one of the most humbling experiences I have faced. I went through a depression within the first several months back home, but within that first year back home, I experienced the Holy Spirit in more ways than I ever have before in my life. The words of the Bible came to life and I would spend hours reading and having such an inspirational understanding of scriptures that I once thought was so confusing.

For everything I suffered while in the New Age, God redeemed me for it: for every nightmare, God has given me a dream about His truth and promises of the future He has for me. For every moment I felt depersonalization, He has given me people who have held my hand and so much joy so I can accept that I am really here and alive.

For every dream I had for success and for a life as an artist, He has given me new dreams and ambitions that come from His own thoughts about me that He has had since before I was even born. And for every moment I felt and heard the ideas of demons, the Holy Spirit came alongside me, even in the dark hours of the night when I could not sleep because of the haunting memories.

He gradually started returning to me memories of my childhood innocence piece by piece when I prayed or read the Bible, even though I thought I could never regain them again. That alone was supernatural, because most of my memories disappeared after the devil attacked me in my room that one night. I left the dance industry of Hollywood, but began creating a dance film in Ohio about my salvation. I left the business I helped run on the beach in California, but God gave me ideas for food and now have started a food business with my mom. I have never experienced a love that was so attentive to every detail of my pain in order to restore every aspect of myself. That is not something a universe can do — only a Person who has an intimate relationship with you can do that. And that Person is Jesus Christ.

2
Testimony

Unconscious Covenants

Saba Tekle

Deuteronomy 18:10–12

There shall not be found among you anyone who burns his son or his daughter as an offering, anyone who practices divination or tells fortunes or interprets omens, or a sorcerer or a charmer a medium or a necromancer or one who inquires of the dead, for whoever does these things is an abomination to the Lord. And because of these abominations, the Lord your God is driving them out before you.

For four or five nights after I left the New Age and gave my life to Christ, I could not sleep. I was experiencing such intense spiritual warfare that I grew afraid of going to sleep due to the attacks and nightmares I was experiencing. As soon as I tried to rest, I would wake up trapped in a lucid dream with a presence that was pure evil. It was so dark that it sent chills down my body. I would try to stay awake at night and sleep during the day until one night I fell asleep due to exhaustion. This time there was not a demonic spirit, it was God. Jesus told me to tell Christians to stop practicing New Age…

Introduction

I never would have thought that I would be writing a book about Jesus or being saved, let alone reciting Bible scriptures. I was usually the youngest and only woman of color at New Age events, courses, and classes. I wanted to learn everything about God, life, and how I could know and control my destiny to be successful. This led me to metaphysical stores, then to numerology and astrological chart readings.

I thought the Bible was too old and that there had to be more to spirituality than Jesus being God and saving us from damnation. This evolved into reading spiritual books. Around 2005, I read, *Many Masters, Many Lives* by Brian L. Weiss and *The End of Karma* by Dharma Singh Khalsa, and *Meditation for Medicine, then Tao: the Pathless Path* by Osho. This all led to listening to radio shows and reading books by Hay House (the largest spirituality-based publishing company). When I finally watched *The Secret* and read *Conversations With God* by Neale Donald Walsh, I was hooked. I felt I found the real answers to life, and there was no turning back. At the time I was a free spirit trying to embrace my "godliness".

It is funny though as I look back, that I found it hard to believe that Jesus is the Son of God but somehow found it more believable that I was a god.

I bit the "apple" and it bit me back.

My introduction to Christianity

Let us back up to the 90s. I was brought up as an Orthodox Christian, but my parents were not hardcore religious. My mom was an inherently good woman who had a way of gently teaching me Biblical things through life experiences. My dad, on the other hand, had a way of teaching me what not to do. He was toxic and an alcoholic. However, Christianity was cultural, so we went to Church. Nothing was reinforced when we got home. Not once did we sit down and read the Bible.

But as far as I can remember, my sister was a Bible-thumping believer. As we got older, my sister started going to a Black-American church. At New Covenant Church, we would have to get up to sing and clap. Sometimes you would see people dance or act wild. It was weird, but my sister was having an experience that I could not relate to or understand. It led her to get saved, and things were never the same. She would try to get us to go back. She would say things like, "Jesus is real," and she would try to share her experiences with us. When I would argue with her, she would counterargue that there was proof that backed the Bible. She told me how there were non-believers and atheists who became believers, like Lee Strobel the author of *The Case For Christ*.

I remember thinking even if the Bible was real, there had to be more.

Turning Point

One day my sister came home from Church and called me and my brother demonic. I do not know if it was what she saw in us or if it was the Church getting to her but this was when I started not to like Christianity.

I was turned off by her heaviness in sharing and her judgments of my brother and my "demonic" ways. My brother and I were both like the Bart Simpson of the family — fun, defiant and disobedient. My sister was more like Lisa — boring, studious and self-righteous. We were family but I was starting to see the divide and it hurt me badly.

"Do you think that I have come to give peace on earth? No, I tell you, but rather division. For from now on in one house there will be five divided, three against two and two against three." - Luke 12:51-53

So I would start to challenge her with, "How is Jesus the Son of God? Aren't we all God's children?" or "If

Jesus is God's Son is He not my brother? How can Jesus be the Son and God at the same time? After that, she stopped talking and it was crickets from then on.

I think I was jealous of Jesus. Why was he so special to God and not us? Not me?

From what I gathered from my own continued search for answers, the most common response from pastors was, "We shouldn't ask such questions."

Hmmmmm....

I would still attend Church (I cannot remember if I had a choice) but it all felt phony. I could sense the Pastor was a fraud. Some years later it came out that he was stealing.

But even while I was straying away, I will never forget the day my sister looked me dead in the eye and said, "One day you will be Christian". That was well over 15 years ago. At the time I had laughed inside because I had a thought that it was she who would not be a Christian anymore.

Even after debates and my denial of Christ, secretly I was battling sin and had no one to turn to. Many nights I would cry myself to sleep, filled with sorrow. I would write poetry to cope with the emotions of being disobedient and sinful. I overall felt like there was a cloud over my head. Being a Christian was culturally infused, so it was hard to walk away completely. I believed there was truth to the Bible — lying or murdering is wrong — but I thought it was wrong to have hell shoved down my throat so I began to create my own beliefs.

I was a "New Ager" before I was officially introduced to the New Age. In other words, I was a progressive lukewarm Christian.

Once I secretly denounced that I was not "Christian *Christian,*" it felt like the cloud lifted. It was somehow easier to not sin because I no longer felt like a pastor was breathing down my neck. Of course, the inner battles did not stop, so I was led even further away from God and further down the New Age spiritual healing path.

My Full Testimony

New Age, Family Drama, and Trauma...

I am sure that it was our family dynamic that led my sister to go to Church and get saved. Our family was so unstable, troubled, and traumatic that for her it called for Jesus. For me it was spiritual and emotional healing.

My parents' marriage was rocky and toxic and every year there was a threat of divorce. Because of it, I struggled with abandonment, neglect, and lack of affection because they were always either away working or the focus was on them working things out between each other. There was love, lots of love, but it was not enough. I had emotional needs that were not being met, like having their presence, or like being comforted or held.

Around this time my sister developed a rare condition and had no treatment options. It was so severe that the doctors even sent her home to die. We had a hospice comfort kit and a pill to give her for when *that time* came. But she miraculously recovered. This still took a toll on my family and affected their attention and focus. Even though I had witnessed the miraculous healing of her body, I did not conclude that Jesus healed emotionally. I was in turmoil. At times I just wanted to die.

When I got past crying about sin, I started to cry myself to sleep due to depression and neglect. When we were not dealing with my parents' toxic relationship, we were dealing with my sister's health scares. The best way to put it was that she was in remission — there is no way to classify it because what she had was so rare. Jesus kept her alive for us, but she was left with random health scares that would still arise.

When we were not dealing with all of that, I dealt with feelings of loneliness and isolation and confusion over how to understand God amid pure chaos.

> *Just because I did not accept Jesus, did not mean I did not acknowledge there is a God.*

But there was another turning point many years later around 2002 that pushed me out, as people would pick up on my self-made beliefs about Christianity. I was told things like, "If you don't believe Jesus is the Son of God, or if you don't believe in the resurrection, then you are not Christian." I felt bullied, so I removed Christianity/Other from my social media page and kept it pushing.

> *Judgments and now bullying… yeah not for me… it seemed there was more emphasis put on what I believed than how we should behave.*

Anywho…I left thinking I could just "earn" my way to Heaven. That God will see all the good I will try to do and accept me anyways… right?

This all morphed into some self-righteous behavior as time progressed and I became toxic and judgmental like the Christians I hated all while being this "free spirit". I did not have peace.

Nothing But New Age and The Downsides

In 2005 I moved to Atlanta to start a career in modeling while simultaneously yearning to know God and desiring inner peace. I was trying to balance the two worlds — being a video girl for music videos and being spiritual.

This was the year I read the books I mentioned at the beginning. This was also the year I started getting my degree in metaphysics and the year that I watched The Secret. This was when my life became nothing but the New Age.

When I learned about the power of thoughts and the law of attraction I was in awe, inspired, and also scared. That same week, I feared my thoughts to the point that when I was driving, I had this fear and thought of "What if someone drove down the wrong side of the street and ran into me?" And guess what? It happened and I had to swerve out of the way to narrowly avoid the crash. It took some time to adjust to the "power of my thoughts" because I also had this fear and thought of "going crazy".

Little did I know those were my 1st demonic attacks.

Later I was introduced to reading, *Conversations With God* by Neale Donald Walsh. Everything seemed to finally become full circle.

"I have come in my Father's name, and you do not receive me. If another comes in his name, you will receive him." - John 4:3

From that book I adopted the beliefs I felt early on in life that there was more than one way to God, there was no such thing as good and evil, there is no hell, you are the creator of your reality, and that we humans are Gods and Goddesses.

Although it affected my life, it did not change my life. I could not "stay positive" to save my life. I found it hard to speak things into existence or manifest through acting because it all felt so deceptive, even though I would try to fight through it.

So this lead me into a search for more answers and practices. I had my breakthrough spiritually as I started to do Yoga, but it was not converting into enlightenment.

Because even following that, I had many dark moments and episodes of challenging moments like panic attacks, getting in fights, and getting booked *(yes, in a holding cell)* for outbursts.

But I continued down this path. I never stopped trying to understand it because I saw how negative thoughts could easily manifest, so soon enough I believed I will get to the positive.

Hindsight is 20/20 so as I look back these were also demonic attacks. But I will dive deeper later... keep reading.

Distaste and No Success

Some time passed and now it's 2008 and I didn't have a breakthrough as far as success in money goes, but this was also during the recession so that *I guess* didn't help. I did get a feeling, from what felt like God, to stop trying to balance both worlds that I was called for more.

At the time I was hanging out with celebrities in nightclubs after dark, but in the morning I was on this search for more meaning, money, and peace. I started to break from that world, as it made me feel empty. I also ended up becoming financially challenged, which forced me to move to Houston where my sister had just moved due to a job promotion.

I was staying with her and she helped me get a job. But she still had health issues so during these times I would share these things with her that she should do for her health (like go see John "Of God", the spiritual healer in Brazil who was later convicted of rape) and she would always refuse and say his way of healing was not Biblical.

I continued to grow my distaste for Christianity. *Why would God not want her to have peace and healing?* I saw my sister miraculously bounce back from her health issues but her episodes were traumatic and what she had was rare, so it felt like death was still lingering.

I would wonder why, why could she not DO anything outside of the Bible. Why didn't God just heal her completely? Why can't she do alternative healing? Why does He want us all to suffer? This made me shy even more away with distaste.

As far as I could see, Christianity was still dividing us, holding us back, and keeping us from things trying to help while Jesus wasn't doing all He could.

I felt so powerless trying help her and help myself. I guess the New Age and self-help made me feel empowered, because even when it wasn't working, it gave me answers.

Work Success and The Downfalls

At my new sales job, things started to get better for me when I would combine personal development and goals. I was having some breakthroughs but it was never enough.

One of the downsides to some of the success I was finally having was dealing with the jealousy and torment I received from my co-workers. This was eye opening. I had thought success was going to make me happy, but the jealousy and petty behavior made me go home and cry myself to sleep or drink to cope. I wanted to do anything but be like them, so I decided to go on a Hay House Cruise after receiving emails from the popular publishing company about the trip. I saw it as a sign to make a change into spiritual and self-help writing as a career.

On that cruise ship, I learned something very eye-opening: that publishing, even though spiritual, was a business. Some of the more accomplished Hay House authors and speakers acted like celebrities, I didn't get it. I thought we were spiritual people, doing "God's" work. *Why did it call for such backwards behavior?*

I got back and had another breakthrough in peace and writing, started a blog, and co-authored a book. I left my job. I was running away from working for other people to become a new age – self-help, spiritual author.

2010 – 2013 - Healing

The next three or four years I worked to build a business and create a spiritual practice.

I got involved with Tibetan singing bowl sound healing and sound baths with crystal bowls; these became part of my practice and were my go-to for both healing and peace.

I even got my sister to come to a session. When we left I asked her, "How do you feel?" She said she was not sure, and that she could not tell if something had left her or came into her.

I loved these sessions and gradually began reading more books about healing. I began practices such as EFT tapping and rewiring old memories, which seemed to work. I would listen to the audio by Deepak Chopra, Marianne Williamson, and Lisa Nichols.

I started to get frustrated because while these practices helped me become peaceful and positive, they were not producing results as far as my finances. Then I was introduced to writing gratitude letters as a spiritual practice. For 30 days I wrote a letter to a spirit guide and soon went from being a struggling spiritual writer and life coach to a spiritual and self-help publisher in Los Angeles.

I began to model my publishing company around Louise Hay's publishing company Hay House. Louise was the owner of the largest spiritual publishing company of our time and I wanted to be like her. I started to create a book series around, "Chicken Soup for the Soul" compiled by one of the teachers of *The Secret*, Jack Canfield.

This all led me to publish a co-authored book series and it had much success. But I had exhausted myself and it was not as fulfilling as it should have been.

Panic Attack a.k.a. Spiritual Awakening a.k.a. Demonic Attack

After years of the ups and downs of building a business, I had a panic attack. It was not my first attack but this one was random and different. At this point in my life, I was into almost all forms of New Age practices and was on the brink of a spiritual awakening.

I was using crystals and tarot cards as well as getting readings. I was doing body code healing, distant healing, and chakra balancing. I traveled to highly spiritual places, like Sedona three times, Joshua Tree three times, and Mount Shasta two Times. I did Ho'oponopono and worked with medical intuition. I was told I was an empath and would need to do clearings and entity removals.

Entities were explained to me as earthbound spirits, they are people who had passed away and have not crossed over. For some reason, I would attract many of these entities and had to consistently get them cleared from my system.

All of these things lead me to a panic attack that felt like the brink of insanity.

I was on the phone with an author friend of mine, who was also a psychic medium, and out of nowhere I started to feel anxiety so high it felt like I was going cray, cray (crazy). I ran out of my apartment and into the parking garage to calm down. Eventually, I got into the tub and took a bath.

After calming down, I did some research and then talked to a friend who was a spiritual advisor. I found out I was having a spiritual awakening. But I also talked to a medical intuitive, who led me to a functional doctor, and found out I had Hashimoto's — an autoimmune disease also known as hypothyroidism. It is not uncommon to have these symptoms with this disease.

What it also felt like was the "ego death" happening all at once. It was disturbing, but my sanity kept holding on thinking there would be a light at the end of the tunnel. There was no light. I had to search for more help which led me to sign up for someone's email list. I learned then and couldn't believe being "awakened" was also a "business". Each day I received an email to do literally one thing. It was torture and it was not until the fourth and fifth day that I got the help I needed. One thing I had to do was remove the crystals from my house to feel better. After the fifth day, I was told to use tea tree oil and then I was sold coaching. *Yikes.*

Each day I felt out of my mind. At night I would feel a sea of energy crashing into me, drowning me and weighing me down.

One day I saw an octopus-like creature floating through my room. I would ignore the feelings and try to ground myself by putting my feet on the grass. It would work temporarily then I was back in the weird spiritual high.

I was also experiencing both derealization and depersonalization. Something I felt when I would have a bad weed high.

Around this time, I found a documentary on Netflix about Osho, a spiritual guru, that had an impact on my life. The documentary was about how his organization's poisoned a community in Oregon and how Osho tried to arrange an assisted suicide. The story got even darker when the leader of his organization tried to kill the person who had attempted to assist in his suicide. Eventually, he *mysteriously* died.

These moments were the first time I saw a New Age or "spirituality" break. I saw the cracks but now the solid ground I thought I was on was breaking open. My foundation was getting shaken up but I was too deep in to see the full picture — that it was all a deception. Also around that time, I saw a video of Doreen Virtue, the highest-selling Hay House author, getting baptized and saved. I did not get it. Also, as famous as she was, I was not into angel cards, fairies, or her books, so it felt like it did not apply to me. *This was a lie that I believed.*

Apparently, at the end of the spiritual awakening, you get a spiritual gift. Mine, I was told, was a mediumship. It made sense considering I frequently dealt with entities. But I ignored it and pretended like the seven days of oppression did not happen. I wanted to return this so-called gift. Even though the major symptoms subsided, from that day on I still suffered from derealization and depersonalization.

That panic attack, Hashimoto's diagnosis, and now mental health symptoms lead me into more New Age practices. I eventually got into past life regression and distance healings that seemed to work to heal from the awakening and health scare. This was to assist with my chronic depression and misery that kept lingering no matter what I dabbled in. I was exhausted.

I can't remember everything I did but I combined spiritual healing and diet to get past it, which also helped with my autoimmune disease. When I got a bit better, I would go to tarot readers for guidance on where I should live or what I should do next. I was told I was ready to move back to LA. I saw a shaman before I decided to leave and she did a ceremony of some sort. I left there with some peace, as she told me that my life would get better if I became a shaman.

I looked into the courses on but becoming a shaman cost $2000, so I picked up a $12 book and could not get into it fully. Back in LA things had not been going my way, and when things wouldn't go my way I would just blamed everything but the problem. I would think I should pick a better reader or even healer next time. *But the problem was the path I was on. It had me going in circles.*

The lies..the lies…we tell ourselves.

The Biggest Turning Point

My biggest turning point is when COVID hit. Just before it hit, I was continually moving because of entities. Entities, remember, were spirits that have not transitioned to God and are trying to find their way back but are earthbound. I was told there were good and bad entities.

I went from working with tarot readers to mostly shamans because shamans had psychic, medium, and healing powers. A friend had recommended a specific shaman to me, and she had me do more clearings and other things that with hindsight make absolutely no sense to me now. For example, this Shaman told me that I was a portal, and then I paid to have my "portal" shut down.

I even attempted to figure out what to do with the medium gift I had, so I hired a shaman to teach me. He told me for 30 days to meditate and do a light breathing exercise. Then I could start communicating with the dead and start what he called, "office hours". In other words, I would choose a time when I would communicate and when I would not. *I found it odd that mediumship and mediation went hand in hand. As well as channeling. Hmmm…*

I left after deciding to not do any of that. When I was told I was an empath, I thought it fit and made sense. When I was told I was clairvoyant, I thought this is cool, but not cool to know people's business. But when I was told I was a medium, I was like… get somebody else to do it. I just wanted to try to figure it out if that is what I was meant to do.

I have been in a new apartment in just a week and I was told to move because of these spirits. Interestingly enough, this particular apartment was next to a Christian Church, *go figure.*

Now prior, when I was told I had entities, I would just believe whoever told me without actually feeling them or seeing the entities. But in this apartment, I could feel them and there were groups of them. Sometimes it felt like I should walk around them. I remember buying a sage kit at House of Intuition (a witch, I mean, a metaphysical store). I started to burn coals, and smoke would fill the entire room, it did nothing but make the room feel even tenser.

Since I had to transition fast, I left everything behind and chose a micro-furnished apartment. It was the size of a shoebox. Then Covid hit and there I was in a tiny apartment with my dog and with a history of a compromised immune system. I was shaken. *At the time if I had died, I surely would have been in Hell.*

Amid the move and working with the shaman, I would sense both good and bad energy. I felt the presence of dark forces come into my space after feeling good. I knew something was off but was afraid to speak up.

My "spiritually enlightened" friends would enable the New Age and offer things like pendulum clearings or say that it was a part of the process. I started to work with another healer to make sure my Hashimoto's was in check. He was also an enabler. For every healing he did, it called for more healing. *This was a trend.*

A year went by and I started to want to work on the underlying depression. So I worked with another body code healer that charged $300 for every 30 min session that incorporated healing with Jesus and I had multiple sessions to figure out the depression and other things left from childhood to heal. All his healing also required more healing. *Go figure.*

OH TULUM

I wanted to turn away from all New Age spiritual healing and get out of America, so I went to Tulum, Mexico. I thought an extended vacation might be all I needed.

I got to Tulum and I went for a walk and found out I was within walking distance of this beautiful spiritual center. They had all types of healing ceremonies, one included a shaman. I thought it was a sign, and after the three hour ceremony, I connected with the shaman who seemed more authentic than the ones I had worked with prior.

We did a few sessions. I even hired him to do distant healing work on a guy I was friends with and talking to - he was my baestie (my bae and best-friend) who was depressed and suicidal.

Unfortunately my baestie ended up being a covert narcissist – the worst type. Covert narcissists manipulate you through their emotions. I was too busy thinking I could help heal him that I did not see it until it was too late.

It seemed at the time we were both having breakthroughs. We had both been suicidal — him more than me — but now we were not. He even flew in and we did a Temazcal healing ceremony that which was a very intense experience. I could not handle being in the sweat hut filled with herbs. I ran out to cry due to it inducing so many emotions. There was a moment of peace after that, which made me feel like it was worth it. He, on the other hand, enjoyed all of it; the healings, cacao heart ceremony, spiritual massage and just before he left we got the OM ॐ symbol tattooed.

Overall, I was starting to experience freedom, happiness, and peace I had been searching for my whole life. Not just working with the shaman, but living in Tulum was so beautiful, heart-centered, and loving.

But Tulum started to get dangerous in more ways than one. In some areas, it was like a death trap as the Airbnbs are deep in the woods with no lighting and poor roads. In other areas, there were Cartel shootings and killings. Tulum is small, so if anything happened, it would happen 15 minutes away from each other. Then there were military and corrupt cops that would scour the neighborhoods. They did not make me feel any safer. It was also expensive to be there.

The beauty of Tulum was captivating. I was especially taken in by the contrast between the chaos of the military men on every corner and the serenity of the ocean views. At the same time, however, whenever I would eat, I would still be hungry, and whenever I would drink, I would still be thirsty. I was satisfied in so many ways, but never fully satiated.

"Jesus said to them, 'I am the bread of life; whoever comes to me shall not hunger, and whoever believes in me shall never thirst.'"

I decided to leave Tulum and stop my escape from depression (also known as my digital nomad adventure) after there were multiple electrical outages. Even the streetlights would go out and no one had answers as to why. One night I felt like I could have easily been a victim to sex trafficking, and after the last fearful night, I left.

When I returned to Los Angeles, the depression came back and it was even greater. I found myself in more situations that did not add up considering the work I had done in Tulum.

My Exit Out Of New Age

When I returned to LA, I was staying with my baestie a.k.a. the CN (covert narcissist), but he was behaving that out integrity, it made me feel unsafe emotionally and/or physically. He had told me his depression and suicidal thoughts were from his ex and past relationships. Yet, his ex would also pop up or stop by to drop off something. He led me believe she was crazy, but he also behaved in ways that clearly triggered her which made me felt uncomfortable. I moved onto yet another apartment, then another apartment, and the last one felt dark, and all of the things felt orchestrated by the Devil.

One night after moving out, the CN and I met up because we had a friendship I thought could be salvaged.

Instead, I walked into his home which seemed staged as if a woman had been there. By the end of the night, I started to see more toxic enticing/drama-inducing behavior, such as he was taking private calls, and texts and then acting like he suddenly had other plans. I could sense that it was all an act to get me to react. I just wanted to go home. I didn't play into it and that is when and why he took it to another level. He tried to kick me out of his car after I said his behavior was shady. As his behavior intensified, I responded by saying, "No wonder your ex wanted to hurt herself."

What I had referred to were the stories that he would share about how his ex would bang her head on the floor or punch herself. But then one day she popped up randomly, I could over hear their conversation and she made a claimed that he hit her. At first I didn't believe her. I thought that she was crazy, but then his behavior made me want question everything. This all made me want to "just die". I was just coming out of the depression, I had helped this man with his own suicidal thoughts, given him my time and bought him things so he could feel better, and yet now he is causing me so much drama. This made more depressed, I even questioned if I wanted to continue living.

I am sure he could tell I was responding without care for him, I was over it. I decided in my mind this will be the last night I will see him. The illusion of thinking he was the victim of his past relationship dropped. He yelled at me, and told me to get out of his car, as I was already trying to leave, he was bullying me, so it ended with me throwing things at him and kicking his car.

How embarrassing. I had thought I was better than this. I had thought I had healed from stuff like this. But when bullied, my traumatized and wired response is to fight back. Things ended up getting even worse. He overcharged me for the damages, cursed me out, and wished I was dead. I had retaliated, but to nowhere near the level that he had.

Please understand that I didn't believe in the Devil, let alone demons, but everything was just so dark that it was hard not to see. I didn't have bad karma up until I reacted that night. My responses have been peaceful or positive. I did engage in sexually immoral behavior, but I didn't see my life as sinful because even then it was in moderation, so I excused it. Aside from that, I kept everything in check, but I one thing I never did was check in with God. You see, when you think you are "God", you think you don't have to repent or that you have someone to answer to.

When you think you are "God" you create your own idea of what is "good or bad" or the consequences thereof. *And I was eventually humbled.*

At that time two other women I was working with (one was a healer/intuitive the other was a psychic) would mention things like narcissism, demons, or the Devil. When it came to him and this court case I was involved in. Around this time I was suing men and the case and everything about the battle was also very dark - I was up against men I am sure were in bed/business with the Devil. But I was never told how to overcome it all. Until I got saved.

"Behold, I give unto you power to tread on serpents and scorpions, and over all the power of the enemy: and nothing shall by any means hurt you. 20 Nevertheless, do not rejoice that the spirits submit to you, but rejoice that your names are written in heaven."

The answers I got from them, dealing with darkness, from the shamans and all, were to move, or they would pretend to do something but nothing would change, say it's because of a past life, or they would say things will work in my favor but it didn't. But sometimes I would get sound advice and wouldn't listen because it didn't make sense. Never once did they say it was from sinning, that I had demons or generational curses. Also no one suggested Christianity as the answer.

It was, in fact, the answer.

My understanding before all of this piling up was that "The universe is a friendly place" – Louise Hay, and that there is no such thing as good and evil. Oh, and if you put out positive energy you will get it back. *YIKES, the lies.* Or that Satan isn't real but my experiences were showing me that the Devil is very much real and I was being targeted.

One of the core traits of narcissistic men is that they hate the good in you, and I would hear how my light irritated their demons. Whatever light I had, it was dimming. I was dwindling and sometimes even drowning in all of this dark energy.

My CC – Jesus and Jesus Alone

I needed more help, and some of my friends were seeing a therapist, so I thought that was what I needed. It turns out that the therapist was a Christian coach. I was never too closed-minded for Christian stuff, but I categorized it as Christ Consciousness or Jesus as a Prophet.

Even my previous healers would mention Jesus and act as if they were healing with Him. I found out that they were not actually saved and what they were doing was not in the Bible. They would incorporate Jesus with other people and spirits that were demonic. My Christian coach was a Bible believer as she would say things like, "Try Jesus and Jesus alone".

Saved by Grace

My Christian coach continued to share that I was mixing too much stuff. I would hear her, but did not quite get it. Then one day she took it a step further and said, "My little love bug, call on the Holy Spirit for 21 days," and then shared a visual I would envision while doing it.

I don't recommend using any visualization while calling on the Holy Spirit, this what was shared starting out.

Before I continue, I want to share the prayer that I believe worked and that set the stage for what happened next, and I also want to share the prayer that did not work.

For one, when I noticed that I still felt lost, even when manifesting success and mixing it with spiritual things that I felt benefited humanity, I started saying the *Course Of Miracles* prayer: "Where would you have me go? What would you have me do? What would you have me say, and to whom?" I was calling on God to lead me, because I did not understand why I was not happy. That prayer never worked.

About three years ago, when things got darker (so dark it was getting easier to deny any God at all), I decided to pray from my heart. I said prayed "God, if there is a Devil, he is going to be waiting for me outside my door. I know you work in mysterious ways, so I ask that you bring me closer because I know it will be easier to fall completely away from you than to believe now that you exist in the midst of all this darkness."

That prayer, years prior, worked because I was carried through those dark times. Around this time, I had stopped writing gratitude letters. These letters were helping be had been helping with my success, but it was all empty manifestations. Yet when I stopped, I did not suffer financially because he carried me and protected me. I was so protected but could not see directly. But now the Devil, bit by bit, was manifesting in different ways. He could no longer hide and in many forms, demons tried to interfere by sending me more false Jesus's. But this coach was the first to say, "Try Jesus and Jesus only," and her beliefs were more based on the Bible.

That day I chose to listen to her because this was the first time I was introduced to the Holy Spirit. Had I known I could call on Him, I would have chosen it over crystals, angels numbers or any false gods any day.

That day I had a moment that changed my life forever.

Holy Spirit

I called on the Holy Spirit and experienced what people call deliverance. I started to hear words come out of my mouth that were not my words. I would shake and immediately it was revealed to me that the shamans did this to me. I had demons that passed down to me through them and from the healing sessions. Each time

I was spiritually open and vulnerable, that let demons in.

One thing you have to understand is that demons come in when you are practicing sin, and since the New Age does not believe in Jesus, shamans will have demons in more ways than one. Those demons will transfer when you open yourself up spiritually to be healed by them or anyone that is not a practicing Christian healing not in Jesus' name.

The second day I did it again and the same thing happened. I would shake and hear words that were not my words and in a voice that was not my voice and knew then I needed to get saved. I needed Jesus to save me from whatever was happening inside of me. I did not know how to explain it to anyone. I started to do research on how to get saved.

I got on my knees and recited the words:

"Father, I come before in the name of Jesus. I recognize I have sinned and I repent. I renounce all my sins. I ask that you completely cleanse me, forgive me, wipe away all my mistakes. Completely erase them. I thank you for that.

And I ask Lord Jesus to be Lord of my life, to be my savior, to come live inside me and make me new. And I thank you Lord as I give you my life, now take it and do something with it.

I surrender to you now. I give you my life right now and I commit my entire life to you. I receive you now in Jesus name. Amen."

On the third night, Jesus came to me through a vision in my heart.

In my heart, it was all white and he was in the middle. It was like he was walking towards me coming from the light. It felt like it was his way to say that he was here, he is coming, and he will restore me and my heart.

What I did not mention is that four nights before, my heart was hardening. I was becoming miserable, not just depressed. There were moments where I felt attacked like I was seeing demonic things. Then I was starting to turn against my sister who grew after I was kicked out of the car by the covert narcissist.

I saw the trend that in my life the people I try to help and save always end up hurting me. I would usually allow it because my upbringing was one where everyone's problems — my parent's relationship, and my sister's health — were greater than mine. So I learned to put others before myself, and usually people would take me for granted. Some would flat-out hurt me. All of this was bubbling up.

But I was immediately relieved. My emotions were healing. Jesus was restoring my heart instantly. But other things lingered like my mental health, depersonalization, and derealization.

Here is why...

Unconscious Covenant With The Devil

Once Jesus revealed himself, I started telling people, and the demons that were still there started to turn on me. They were already turning on me, but now they could no longer do it in the dark. When Jesus steps in, the light shines in all the darkness including all the New Age practices I did that let the demons in.

What I learned is that these demons still had legal grounds to attack me. Legal grounds means they have rights. When you invite them in, that is how you come into covenant with them. I had unconsciously come into covenant with the Devil through New Age beliefs and practices.

Basically, it was now being revealed that they were under contract to oppress, suppress and even attack my life. I had to denounce and repent every word or deed that gave them grounds, if I did not, they could do anything to torment me.

These demons were attacking me all this time, but this time it was obvious because the gig was up. I knew exactly what they were and what they were here to do. I found out later that I was chosen to expose them. The dark side knows God's plans for us and they will try to interfere with those plans in any way they can.

A Message From God

Shortly after Jesus revealed himself, I started the process of moving out of my third dark and demonic apartment. I headed out to Palm Springs where I purchased a rental property, and it was there I began the worst spiritual warfare to date.

My anxiety started to hit an all-time high. I was not eating the best foods, but I knew there was more to it. To help with my transition out of the New Age, I started joining Facebook support groups.

There I found Joscelyn, the co-author of this book, in a group. I started watching her YouTube Podcast at the time called "Not Milk" — a show exposing things in the New Age, how not to fall into deception and how to become a better Christian.

I began to reach out to her as things progressed to get guidance about what I had been feeling and I started to talk to a real therapist. I did not go back to my Christian Coach even though she helped me to this point. I did not get why she did not prepare me and I assumed she either did not know what she was doing or knew nothing of true spiritual warfare.

Spiritual warfare for some could mean an argument, blow up, loss of job, illness, accident, incident, or a timeline of these events happening repeatedly. But at this time, I was actually experiencing the spirits and demons behind them that either orchestrates them or causes them.

My anxiety was getting so bad that I could not sleep. Then when I would sleep, I would get attacked by the demons and would have nightmares, each one darker than the last. It felt like they had the power to hurt me if I fell asleep. This happened every night, so I would stay awake all night and sleep during the day. I bought a cross, and a physical and audio Bible and kept them next to me. After the fourth or fifth night of spiritual warfare, due to exhaustion, I did sleep soundly and that is when I received a message from God.

Tell Christians to stop practicing New Age.

"What about the people in the New Age? Do I try to stop them as well?" I replied.

It is important but not as important as warning Christians.

Yes, God.

It happened so fast. There was a knowing that it was God and his message was clear but when I got up, *I still questioned, was it really him?*

When you experience the warfare I experienced, you know the last thing those demons want is for others to stop being deceived. It was like they knew God would come in a dream so they did not want me to sleep.

But let me backup a bit. My anxiety was keeping me from leaving the house. Everything seemed scary. I would walk my dog real quick and head back. Things started to turn for the worse when I would call on the Holy Spirit and this time I started to hiss like a snake. I was shaken. I stopped calling on Him and tried to take breaks on all things Christian.

That did not help. Everything took a tipping point when I had an anxiety attack and had to call an ambulance to get me to get out of the house.

It was suggested I get delivered, like a full on deliverance, but the research I was doing on it and the feedback from Joscelyn and then others was mixed. Joscelyn had had several deliverances and was for it. Apparently, Doreen Virtue, who also has a YouTube show, had one and it made her worse. I even reached out to her and her response was to read the Bible. So there was a divide now in Christianity.

I still could not rest, so I decided to have my first deliverance. I was asked to wait in the Church as I waited to be seen. But these demons would not even let me wait in the Church. Everything made me feel crazy. I was finally seen, and the demons began to manifest.

In the New Age, the only time I would hear the word manifest was referring to money, but in Christianity, it is used to describe how Jesus would show up OR when a demon would act out and show itself.

"He who has My commandments and keeps them, it is he who loves Me. And he who loves Me will be loved by My Father, and I will love him and manifest Myself to him."- John 14:21

Now the demons began to talk. They would say things like, "I am going to make her crazy," "I am going to make her kill herself" and even one tearfully said, "I have been with her too long, she won't know who she is without me."

One of them was right. I did not know who I was, but there was no turning back. I was lost in uncharted territory, far from land, far from who I was, but I trusted I would find a new home in me with Jesus navigating me now.

The women helping with the deliverance asked me if I threw away everything that was New Age, and I said, "Yes, I began that process a while back and I even felt better when I did," but they told me to ask Jesus if there was more. He did show me more things, like a $2000 + painting that was religious but not Christian.

"The images of their gods you are to burn in the fire. Do not covet the silver and gold on them, and do not take it for yourselves, or you will be ensnared by it, for it is detestable to the Lord your

God. Do not bring a detestable thing into your house or you, like it, will be set apart for destruction. Regard it as vile and utterly detest it, for it is set apart for destruction." - Deuteronomy 7:25-26

One person helping with the deliverance asked if I did Kundalini Yoga — that was the serpent spirit causing me the most problems and together we all prayed to get it out. This was the scariest and most traumatic experience of my life.

When I returned home, I threw away or burned whatever was left that was New Age including the painting, but I can tell things were still undone. I knew there was more, and at random times more demons would manifest because I still had so many open doors due to old beliefs and practices I had done.

I asked Jesus why he would allow this, and He showed me that each time, I was warned. A memory flashed before my eyes of when my sister told me it was demonic. I understood and knew. He was still here, and had always been here, to help me fight through it.

Jesus warns through people, take heed.

I was not looking forward to another deliverance. I learned I needed to be careful of who I worked with, who I let lay hands on me or who I had pray for me, but the manifesting continued and I did not care who or what delivered me.

They were trying to make me go crazy and tell me to hurt people including myself. I started to have an anxiety attack to the point where I called an ambulance. I also called my sister and she flew in immediately. When I checked out of the hospital, I checked into a hotel thinking the spirits would just be at my house waiting, but, no, they were in the hotel with me, tormenting me. I started to reach out to everyone I could think of who was a Christian and pleaded for prayer. I then reached out to Derek LaFleur, someone that was connected to me through Jocelyn.

I DMed him and asked for prayer. We got on Facetime and he was preparing to do a deliverance. He got another person on Facetime, Chris Ullery, and they both started to tag-team on my demons.

All of this was happening when my sister was arriving.

They called out spirits according to my practices like shamanism. They called out Jezebel, Baal, and Leviathan (spirit husband). After they would cast them out, Chris and Derrek would circle back because apparently they can hide, or it can be a process due to the layers of how deep I was in the New Age.

I had to repent and renounce spirit guides, spirit animals, soul contracts, witchcraft, mercury retrograde, and more and more things.

Each demon had a story on how they came in — one through being cursed through my bloodline by gossip, another through watching scary stories on Youtube, another through shamans. Some said they were not going anywhere. Others said they would come back through a family member. This took hours upon hours.

Then my sister was almost at my house, so I started to head home in the midst of Facetime. I reached her and told her how weird and scary this all was and that she should go somewhere until we finished.

She said no, she was not afraid.

Neither of us was introduced to deliverance prior, and only a few times did we experience demonic things. Once when we were in the hospital she said she saw the spirit of death walk by and from then on she was not afraid.

So we both entered my home and continued the deliverance.

The Fight To Be Christian Continues

Please keep in mind I never read the Bible and most Scripture I had read was filtered through the metaphysics or the New Age version of Jesus, so it was cherry-picked to manipulate or was passed down through people. So when they would name demons and they would manifest I did not know a single one except for the Jezebel as it was mentioned in movies. Even then I did not think much until she laughed at how she had me going in circles and taunted my tag-team demon slayers and called them names. She was the hardest next to the Kundalini serpent. Every time a demon left, it felt like they were trying to take my mind with them.

Forgiveness was a huge part of the deliverance. I remember thinking that I thought I forgave, but I was in so much pain. *Then I also realized that true forgiveness also comes through Jesus.*

After six or so hours they decided it would be an ongoing deliverance because they could not identify all of the demons. But then we moved to baptism and cleansing of my home from more New Age things.

My sister said years ago that I would be Christian, right about everything our whole life and now I am saved, and we are casting out all my demons and then we got baptized together. Now we are throwing away all of the things that the demons attached themselves to, the demons she had warned me about. It was then that I understood and saw Jesus as a protecting loving Father, as well as the only true and living God. The Holy Spirit revealed things I needed to throw away like family cursed heirlooms, a gift from the covert narcissist, and other expensive things. I did not care what I needed to throw away. OUT IT ALL WENT.

I deleted every New Age email I received. There were so many emails that I deleted and removed myself from the email account altogether. I deleted my browser history, every bookmark, which had sinful things like porn. I removed 98% of Facebook likes which were New Age related.

I removed all the titles of the success I accomplished with my New Age books. I even emailed HuffPost to remove blogs that featured an interview I did with spiritual author Neale Donald Walsh and others. I also emailed Essence Magazine and had them remove a part of a blog I shared that had a New Age practice. Some of this was done after the deliverances.

The fight to be Christian continued and more spirits were revealed, like the spirit of antichrist.

Every day my sister and I would speak in tongues, call on the Holy Spirit, and pray to get all the demons and spirits out. Theses spirit included of death, division, familiar spirits, the spirit of rebellion, python and more.

I remember demons screaming at my first Bible study, yelling, "NOooooooooooooooooo, nooooooooooooo." *If Bible study made them this mad, BIG MAD, I must be on the right path. There was no turning back.*

I thought I would never get through this. I was scared to be alone. Then my sister said that God said she would be going home and I would not be going with her and that we would see His mighty hand at work even while she was gone.

She left, and by His grace I have been strong to this day.

Some days I feel weak, but I get strength and am guided by the Holy Spirit and by the word of God that I read daily which fulfills me.

God took away all desires to sin *(of course there are still temptations)* and I have not needed healing since. Just work and restoration from the trauma of the New Age and sometimes the continuing casting out of demons. I had to get a few more deliverances but now I have learned to do on my own in Jesus' mighty name.

"I love you, O LORD, my strength. The LORD is my rock and my fortress and my deliverer, my God, my rock, in whom I take refuge, my shield, and the horn of my salvation, my stronghold. I call upon the LORD, who is worthy to be praised, and I am saved from my enemies. The cords of death encompassed me; the torrents of destruction assailed me; the cords of Sheol entangled me; the snares of death confronted me. In my distress I called upon the LORD; I cried for help. From his temple he heard my voice, and my cry to him reached his ears." - Psalm 18

Notice how nowhere in the story I shared that I went to God for help when in the New Age? Only what, twice? I went to shamans, tarot readers, healers, self-help books, etcetera, but not God. Well, that was the plan.

The Devil wants you to believe in negative thinking so you are to blame for what his demons do and he wants you to believe in positive energy because he knows positive vibes or thinking cannot defeat him. And vibes lie because the Devil can disguise himself as an angel of light.

Only Jesus can defeat him, only Jesus has defeated him and only Jesus can give us the power to defeat all of them. No one goes to the Father, God, without Him.

But when we engage in sin or operate in practices outside the Bible, we are not protected. We are protected when we obey, when we repent (ask for forgiveness and turn away) and when we renounce (take away their legal ground) then we can rebuke (cast the demons out) in Jesus' mighty name.

Jesus wants a personal relationship with you. He has a plan and that is why the Lord's prayer is THY will, HIS will be done — not YOUR will. His time, not your time He is your Father and a Father protects, provides, and guides. Only under His obedience is He able to.

'Our Father in heaven, hallowed be your name. Your kingdom come, your will be done, on earth as it is in heaven. Give us this day our daily bread, and forgive us our debts, as we also have forgiven our debtors. And lead us not into temptation, but deliver us from evil."

3

New Age VS Christianity

In this chapter, Joscelyn and Saba break down how the New Age opposes Christianity.

To really understand how dangerous and deceptive the New Age is, we are going to break down its history, where it came from and how its core beliefs go against Scripture.

First, New Age spirituality is a melting pot, so there is no universal, exact definition of it. Essentially, it is a combination of eastern religions (i.e. Hinduism, Buddhism, Taoism, etc.) with mysticism and universalism which believes that ascension through enlightenment will cause one to be free from the ego and all religion, then ascend from the 3rd dimension (3D) to the 5th dimension.

To expand further, New Agers believe that all religions are man-made and invented to keep the human race bound and divided, and unable to come to the true knowledge of who they truly are — "gods and goddesses".

The revelation that all religions are essentially the same and that transcending all religions by understanding that we all are, in fact, the Universe and the source of all life, is an essential aspect of the New Age. However, this is directly contradicted by New Age practices themselves.

New Agers incorporate rituals and ceremonies of multiple religions, although their main claim is that New Age is not a religion in itself. Because of this belief, they especially shun the Christian way of life, which is based on the belief that Jesus is the only way, the truth, and the life (the way to Heaven).

"Jesus said to him, 'I am the way, the truth, and the life. *No one* comes to the Father except through me." -John 14:6

Here is a breakdown of each eastern belief incorporated into the New Age:

Hinduism is the belief in reincarnation and karma - the universal law of cause and effect. The main practice includes yoga and other forms of yoga like Kundalini or Hot (Bikram) yoga. Hindus believe that Yoga is an important practice that helps them to be close to Brahman, their god. According to www.hinduwebsite.com, Brahman is "a very mysterious Being".

*"In Hinduism, Kundalini (in Sanskrit it means coiled **snake**) is a form of divine feminine energy (or Shakti) believed to be located at the base of the spine." -Wikipedia*

Buddhism is a non-theistic religion (no belief in a creator or in God). Buddhists believe in the teachings of Buddha, who himself rejected the idea of a creator. Their practices are chanting and meditating. There are shrines and places of worship where Buddha statues are placed for gratitude.

"Buddhists will often bow towards altars or images of the Buddha or a bodhisattva, towards monastics, a religious teacher, relics or objects...

...Many Buddhist practices are done as part of devotion and veneration. The most common types of veneration practices include merit-making, bowing, giving offerings, chanting, meditating on the qualities embodied by specific buddhas and pilgrimage." - Cultural Atlas

Taoism is a Chinese philosophy and religion that believes in living in harmony and balance with the universe. It was loosely based on a mythical figure named Laozi. Taoist practices include meditation, ritual, and martial arts. Taoist rituals involve purification, meditation and offerings to deities. They perform rituals to restore order to the universe and ask the gods to bring peace and prosperity to the village.

Are you seeing the contrast and contradiction between it all? It is confusing, isn't it? Guess who is the author of the confusion? The Devil. Whether it is the basics of the beliefs or the practices themselves, it opposes Jesus' teaching. It is a sin to practice New Age because it goes against the first and second commandments.

1. *I am the LORD your God: you shall not have Gods before me.*

2. *Thou shalt not make unto thee any graven image*

    A graven image is an idol—an object or image, such as a statue, that is worshiped as the representation of a deity or god.

History

The merging of multiple belief systems, thus multiple gods and practices, can be dated as far back as Biblical times, before the coming of Jesus Christ, which makes this concept far from new. The worship of the planets, especially the sun, and multiple gods was common, as well as the beliefs in sexual freedom, perversion, and obtaining more knowledge to ascend to the gods.

This is our modern-day astrology and the incorporation of shaman and witch rituals New Agers do with the New Moons, Solstices and times of the day. This current New Age spirituality is no different than these ancient religions of Sumeria, Babylon, and Canaan, as even the most prominent theosophists in history have acknowledged.

To put it simply, the New Age is as old as Adam and Eve. In other words, it should be considered as the "forbidden fruit" as referenced in the Bible.

In the New Age, a "Third Eye Awakening" is the process of a spiritual awakening that causes one to ascend into spiritual revelation, wisdom, and insight, which results in supernatural abilities, specifically related to spiritual sight. Kundalini Awakening, as mentioned previously, is an extension of this, but includes ascension of the rest of the natural and spiritual senses with the rest of the soul. Oftentimes, people are not warned of the actual dangers of this occurrence, which include the experiences we have mentioned in our testimonies.

New Age spiritual healers claim that the traumatic, demonic symptoms of sexual trauma and perversion from otherworldly entities, uncontrollable astral projection (soul separating from the body), uncontrollable body movements, psychotic episodes, etc., are due to the person's lack of preparation for the awakening. However, even those who do not experience the extremities mentioned above and in our testimonies during either of these awakenings, still experience the evil side of the process.

This is because these practices were created from channeled demonic information and allow a person to get possessed by demons. Kundalini awakening also always includes sexual symptoms, because it relies on the energy that is emitted from the sexual organs. Spiritualists will advise having a shaman to guide you and to practice grounding rituals, which were also rituals we attempted in our experiences that led to more demonic oppression. How can the New Age claim to be about universal love, but the practices necessary to ascend to this "love" require brain-altering trauma, demonization, and torment?

This is why God warned Adam and Eve from the beginning about opening their eyes. Obtaining spiritual knowledge apart from the ways of God will never just be "good", it will include evil knowledge as well that ultimately causes death. The wisdom and knowledge that comes from the Holy Spirit will not require you to be traumatized sexually or possessed by demons.

1 Corinthians 2:12: Now we have received, not the spirit of the world, but the Spirit who is from God, that we might know the things that have been freely given to us by God.

In the Garden of Eden, Adam and Eve were in the presence of God every day. They were made in the image of God, and had their own roles in the Garden. Because they listened to a serpent that mixed lies with truth which appealed to their carnal desire to ascend,

Adam and Eve traded the most valuable position in life they could ever possess for a partial truth — knowing good and evil.

The problem with knowing good and evil is that we as humans are tempted.

James 1: 13: *"When tempted, no one should say, 'God is tempting me.' For God cannot be tempted by evil, nor does he tempt anyone."*

"God can know good and evil and not be tempted because there is no darkness found in Him." (1 John 1:5) *"This darkness is any area in our lives that tends toward rebellion against God, and God cannot rebel against Himself because He cannot deny Himself."* (2 Timothy 2:13)

The fact that Eve even allowed the serpent (Satan) to warp her perception of God's truth in His own words was darkness. This led to more darkness — the desire to become like God, more specifically, to partake in His divine power.

We are still falling for this lie today, and if we pursue the knowledge of good and evil, and any spiritual knowledge apart from the one true God's order, the high price we will pay is eternal death — Hell.

Who brought the New Age here

Helena Blavatsky (also known as Madame Blavatsky), was a Russian mystic, who was considered the godmother of the New Age as she was the first woman to bring the combination of beliefs (Theosophy, later called New Age) to America. Theosophy incorporated Neoplatonism, western esotericism, Buddhism, and Hinduism. Helena also brought Satanism and Occultism; she also ran a magazine called Lucifer.

As stated in the Nordic Journal of Comparative Religion, "H. P. Blavatsky's influential *The Secret Doctrine* (1888), one of the foundation texts of Theosophy, contains chapters propagating an unembarrassed Satanism. Theosophical sympathy for the Devil also extended to the name of their journal Lucifer, and the discussions conducted in it. To Blavatsky, **Satan is a cultural hero**."

The logo for the Theosophical Society, founded by Madame Blavatsky, brought together various ancient symbols. This included a ***snake*** that wrapped around all of them.

Alice Bailey was also one of the first women to write and officially use the term "New Age". She published 24 books on Theosophy under "Lucifer Publishing Company" which later changed to Lucis. Some of her books include: *Discipleship in the New Age, Letters on Occult Meditation, Esoteric healing,* and *Astrology.*

Alice also created the concepts for the New World Order.

We are going to go into why this is problematic... if you already can't tell...

New Agers like to classify themselves as being spiritual and non-religious to imply and impose a sense of humanity and inclusivity, but it is an illusion. Free thinking isn't quite free thought. It is more a planning out of the device for a more deceptive Satanic plan of the New World Order. Don't take my word for it, just keep reading...

Alice Bailey created a 10-point strategy for the New World Order. Here are just the first six points:

- Take God and prayer out of the Education System

- Reduce parental authority over the children

- Destroy the Judeo-Christian family structure

- If sex is free, then make abortion legal and make it easy

- Make divorce easy and legal to free people from the idea of marriage for life

- Make homosexuality an alternative lifestyle

- Alice Ann Bailey (June 16, 1880 – December 15, 1949)

Babylon

In the Bible, it states that there is nothing new under the sun. So let's dive into the roots from where most of this stems. Many won't comprehend this but we are repeating history and starting with Babylon and the Tower of Babel.

Babylon contained some of the earliest occult magic knowledge known to man. In addition to their divination and polytheism of multiple Baals (lords) and significant gods like Ishtar and Marduk, they engaged in perverse sexual rituals to receive blessings from their gods, especially pertaining to the prosperity of their crops. Their practices of divination and occult knowledge led to what we know today as the "Mystery Religions", which envelopes any cult that has secret or hidden wisdom and knowledge (i.e. freemasonry, The Cult of Thelema, the Cult of Dionysus, Ordi Templi Orientus, etc.).

In more recent years, Babylon, or Babalon, has been changed to be considered an actual goddess according to the well-known Satanist and occultist, Aleister Crowley. This goddess is the same one mentioned in Revelation:

Revelation 17:1-2: *One of the seven angels who had the seven bowls came and said to me, "Come, I will show you the punishment of the great prostitute, who sits by many waters. With her the kings of the earth committed adultery, and the inhabitants of the earth were intoxicated with the wine of her adulteries."*

According to Crowley and his channeled writings, Babalon is the epitome of the sexually-freed woman, and is also known as "Mother Earth". This term is also translated to Gaia, the goddess that is channeled in New Age ayahuasca ceremonies and has taken on many forms since ancient times.

One example, Ashtoreth/Asherah (Jeremiah 44 and Judges 10:6-10) is a rendition of this "Mother Earth" goddess and was considered the consort (wife) to Baal. Worship to her was in the form of prostitution, fortune-telling, bestiality, and child sacrifice to name a few. In various cultures, she has been depicted as being androgynous and a goddess of love, fertility, prostitutes, and even war.

Deuteronomy 18:10-14: *Let no one be found among you who sacrifices their son or daughter in the fire, who practices divination or sorcery, interprets omens, engages in witchcraft, or casts spells, or who is a medium or spiritist or who consults the dead. Anyone who does these things is detestable to the LORD; because of these same detestable practices the LORD your God will drive out those nations before you.*

Since the fall in the Garden of Eden, each of us are born in sin, with the knowledge of good and evil. The occult practices have been done since ancient Babylon, Egypt, Sumeria, etc., and are the repercussions of journeying deeper into the knowledge, which can only be done with the aid of demons and Satan himself. One of the greatest lies the occult tells humanity, whether in its "lighter" forms of New Age spirituality (coined "sugar coated" satanism), or in its greater forms such as the Kabbalah, Satanism, or Theosophy, is this:

The more (1) knowledge of good and evil you obtain and the more (2) temptations you create within yourself and give in to, the more you will ascend to godhood.

This is the complete opposite of God's plan for us. The more spiritual knowledge you seek apart from Him, the more you will descend away from His presence.

Matthew 18:2-4: *Then Jesus called a little child to Him, set him in the midst of them, and said, "Assuredly, I say to you, unless you are converted and become as little children, you will by no means enter the kingdom of heaven. Therefore whoever humbles himself as this little child is the greatest in the kingdom of heaven.*

Jesus Christ has called us to become like little children, without the haughtiness of our own minds. Children live under the authority of their parents, without a concern, or ability, or desire for obtaining deep, "hidden" knowledge about the universe. A child's main desire is love and acceptance, and that is cultivated when living in a household of order, not in a household where love is a subjective concept, emotion, or something that must be earned and supernaturally understood through works or rituals. This principle is the same as the one held in the Kingdom of Heaven, because the family dynamic is a reflection of our relationship to God. His desire for intimacy with us is so great, He made reunion with Him over time more simple and for everyone: by grace through faith in Jesus Christ alone (Ephesians 2:8-9).

The sin which we were born in tempts us, and God has called us to resist temptation. The more we resist the temptation that is according to the fleshly nature and darkness in us which desires to rebel against God, the closer we get to His presence.

Matthew 4:10-11: *Then Jesus said to him, "Away with you, Satan! For it is written, 'You shall worship the Lord your God, and Him only you shall serve.' " Then the devil left Him, and behold, angels came and ministered to Him.*

The three temptations Jesus faced in the desert from Satan were all temptations to engage in witchcraft — manipulation of forces or plans ordained by God apart from His will and His order. These three forms of temptation are the main ones that cause people to be attracted to divination and the occult knowledge originating in Babylon:

1. **Manipulation of matter** - *Matthew 4:3: "Now when the tempter came to Him, he said, 'If You are the Son of God, command that these stones become bread.'"*

In Babylonian custom, they believed sexual rituals would cause rainfall for their crops, thus manipulating matter. Shamans in ancient China performed sacrificial rain dance ceremonies as well as Native Americans. We also see these magical practices of manipulating matter in the use of meditation practices to create counterfeit placebo physical healing or the practice of levitation in Buddhist monks.

2. **Manipulation of relationships** - *Matthew 4:5-6: "Then the devil took Him up into the holy city, set Him on the pinnacle of the temple, and said to Him, "If You are the Son of God, throw Yourself down. For it is written: 'He shall give His angels charge over you,' and, 'In their hands they shall bear you up, Lest you dash your foot against a stone.'"*

In this second temptation, Satan tempted Jesus to manipulate His relationship with the Father when jumping from the top of the temple by manipulating the promise of protection, since it was before Jesus' ordained time and way to die. Satan was propositioning Jesus to take advantage of the grace and covenants of God, because of their relationship as Father and Son (although they are still One according to the Trinity).

Some of the main reasons we see many women turning to witchcraft now more than ever are because they are seeking the knowledge of spells and potions to manipulate a man into desiring them - to take advantage of a relationship with them. There are countless cases of shamans charging extreme amounts of money to manipulate clients into constantly paying for healing rituals, without any true healing occurring. All of these are forms of manipulation or taking advantage of someone's rightful desire or will in relation to you, and thus is a form of witchcraft.

3. **Manipulation of future events** - *Matthew 4:8-9: "Again, the devil took Him up on an exceedingly high mountain, and showed Him all the kingdoms of the world and their glory. And he said to Him, 'All these things I will give You if You will fall down and worship me.'"*

One of the greatest versions of this form of witchcraft we see today is the use of manifestation. Countless people in the United States are using manifestation practices to obtain their desired career or financial wealth.

However, as we can see from this passage, receiving earthly prosperity apart from God's will and order will require two things: 1. the "falling down" of your identity, demoting yourself from the Kingdom of Heaven and rejecting your own inheritance as a Child of God, and 2. the worship of the counterfeit, Satan. This is why manifestation practices become so addictive and come with an exaltation and obsession within oneself of the world and its power, along with more potent divination abilities.

Manipulation to gain or use the power reserved to God Himself is also portrayed in the story of the Tower of Babel.

*Genesis 11:1-4: "Now the whole earth had one language and one speech. And it came to pass, as they journeyed from the east, that they found a plain in the land of Shinar, and they dwelt there. Then they said to one another, 'Come, let us make bricks and bake them thoroughly.' They had brick for stone, and they had asphalt for mortar. And they said, 'Come, let us build ourselves a city, and a tower whose top is in the heavens; **let us make a name for ourselves**, lest we be scattered abroad over the face of the whole earth.'"*

The Hebrew word for "name" (shêm) translates to "renown", which is used in Genesis 6:4 in reference to the Nephilim, or "men of renown". These men of renown were the offspring of the humans who had sexual relations with the fallen angels, the ones who rebelled against God. There is speculation on whether the term in this passage "Sons of God" were actually fallen angels. However, there is extensive support for the concept of these divine beings breeding with humans just from the original language of Hebrew and then to

Greek alone. One of them is the fact that the term "Sons of God" is only used in reference to angels in the Old Testament, and isn't used to refer to saved believers until the New Testament.

These, fallen ones had brought occult knowledge and extreme sexual perversion to the generations during the days of Noah. With this understanding, we realize that the people who made the tower of Babel didn't want to simply "make a name" for themselves in plain English terms. They wanted to ascend and merge with the fallen ones, to be like God.

The word that the serpent told Eve initially in the garden was never completely fulfilled, so it left the people who fed into their rebellious, fleshly desires in a constant search and pursuit of the serpent's promise to be fulfilled. This is still happening today. Millions of people are caught in the cycle of working and striving to see the fulfillment of that promise told by Satan that we would "be like God", by pursuing knowledge, spiritual ascension, and success. The common thing you might hear is people want to "make a name for themselves".

We were not created to understand or experience someone not keeping their word because we were created by the Word of God, because the Word was God Himself, and He never breaks his promises (John 1:1,

Numbers 23:19). Therefore, the more we reject Jesus Christ, the more we will work and sin to keep trying to find the result of being "like God".

However, the hunger or need to "make a name" for ourselves is fulfilled by the revelation of Jesus Christ.

Revelation 2:17: *"He who has an ear, let him hear what the Spirit says to the churches. To him who overcomes, I will give some of the **hidden manna** to eat. And I will give him a white stone, and on the **stone a new name written** which no one knows except him who receives it."*

The desire for hidden knowledge comes from a place in our hearts that is an empty well, desperately in need of the reunion with Jesus Christ. This is why He promises to give us the "hidden manna", as referenced in the above scripture, as He is also the bread of life.

We have perverted our own need for personal intimacy with God, with the need for things that are hidden (occult means "hidden"), but Jesus Christ fulfills us in a way where we will not crave nor need to search for the hidden knowledge that never satisfies.

John 6:35: *"Then Jesus declared, 'I am the bread of life. Whoever comes to me will never go hungry, and whoever believes in me will never be thirsty'."*

As shown in Revelation 2:17, Jesus Christ promises to give us a "new name written which no one knows except him who receives it". Instead of giving us hidden knowledge or a name of "renown", which is what Satan and his New Age occult practices promise, Jesus gives us a new NAME — a name that gives us our true identity, precious and intimate between us and our Heavenly Father. That is truly the only knowledge we need, the knowledge of Jesus Christ and the new identity He gives us — an identity and name that does not need to be famous by receiving the affirmation and glory from man or the world, as the men of renown did. It is a name and identity written on a white stone, a stone of purity that is already formed by Him, eliminating our need to create our own brick to create a tower, as the workers did at the Tower of Babel.

As you can see, contrary to what New Agers believe about a controlling God, God did not scatter the people of Babylon to stop them out of sheer abusive control. He scattered them because their ascension would have led to the complete destruction of His creation, and the most unfathomable evil that could have ever existed.

Today, we are seeing the attempt to unify all the languages — or religions — of people all around the world through the belief in New Age spirituality, which is extremely dangerous. People in the New Age are united in the desire and goal to ascend and become Godlike.

So what were the results of the occult practices and sexual perversions of Babylon, and the pursuit of ascension at the Tower of Babel? Death, insanity, shame, and confusion.

In the Old Testament, there are numerous stories of God using His chosen people to destroy the kings of Babylon and their idols. Jezebel, the queen of Babylon, died a horrific death after enforcing Babylonian witchcraft in Israel. King Nebuchadnezzar, who exalted himself above God, lost his mind and behaved like an animal for seven years, leaving him in horrendous shame (Daniel 4). At the tower of Babel, God scattered all the builders of the tower, caused them to each speak a different language, and thoroughly confused them.

In Closing...

Isaiah 47:13–15 NIV: *"All the counsel you have received has only worn you out. Let your **astrologers** come forward, those stargazers who make predictions month by month, let them save you from what is coming upon you. Surely they are like stubble; the fire will burn them up.* ***They cannot even save themselves from the flame... Each of them goes on in his error; there is not one that can save you.****"*

Whether it is astrology, tarot, shamanism, New Age-ism, cleansing rituals, psychic readings, or yoga, it is clear in the Bible that our Heavenly Father does not want you to believe or practice these things. There are ancient spirits and demons attached, and when practiced you come into covenant with them.

In the New Age, the ideal for humanity is "open mindedness", or free spirit, free will, free thought, free love, and free sex, but it is all a mask for the spirit of rebellion and antichrist. It is dangerous, demonic, damaging and destructive and it can cost you your salvation.

"Beloved, do not trust every spirit but test the spirits to see whether they belong to God, because many false prophets have gone out into the world. This is how you can know the Spirit of God: every spirit that acknowledges Jesus Christ come in the flesh belongs to God, and every spirit that does not acknowledge Jesus does not belong to God. This is the spirit of the **antichrist** that, as you heard, is to come, but in fact is already in the world."* - John 4:1-6

For every counterfeit spiritual practice rooted in darkness, there is the true, original version out of God's intent for humanity. For example, shamans, or witchdoctors, are prominent figures in the New Age movement and will lead whole congregations in teaching, counterfeit healings, and psychic readings. However, in the body of Christ, we have the Holy Spirit, baptism, praise and worship, prophesying among other spiritual gifts, and deliverances.

- The Holy Spirit guides and leads us into all truth

- Baptism cleanses us and is a public declaration of our entering into a new covenant with Jesus Christ

- Praise and/or worship can lift us up, deliver and protect us from demons. Reading the Bible with the guidance of the Holy Spirit can as well.

- Pastors and Holy Spirit-led/gifted men and women can prophesy over your life so that you can know God's plan.

- Pastors and/or Holy Spirit led/gifted men and women can facilitate deliverance by the power of the Holy Spirit anytime you are led astray and close doors opened to the dark side. *Please use discernment also pray and ask for guidance from the Holy Spirit on who to go to.*

Further, because the Holy Spirit is freely given to all who believe, any of us, and ALL of us, are called to deliverance and are given spiritual gifts as He wills, not just pastors (1 Corinthians 12:7-12).

This path is rewarding and all that is asked from you is your obedience.

Jesus says: *"If you love Me, keep My commandments ... He who has My commandments and keeps them, it is he who loves Me ... If anyone loves Me, he will keep My word; and My Father will love him, and We will come to him and make Our home with him."*- John 14:15-24.

In the New Age, love is considered to be a high-frequency vibration (432 hz) that is open to our interpretation and is the life force behind our own divine nature. There is no distinct God because all of the universe and God are equal and the same. Because those deceived by the New Age doctrine have no clear definition of God and have equated themselves to God, their definitions and portrayals of love are perverted.

God's definition of love is based on will and principle — His holiness. The Greek word used in John 14 for love is agapē, which is a sacrificial love that seeks the well-being of the other individual. There are other areas in New Testament scripture that use the emotional form of love that is in the context of brotherly affection, which is the word phileō. In the world today, love is defined by phileō and especially the romantic/sexual love (which, in Greek, would be eros instead of phileō) that God ordained between husband and wife. In the New Age, the concept of this impersonal, universal love that primarily comes from self-love, is a perversion that leads to other perversions, because the foundation of Love is in the Father Himself.

1 John 4:8: "He who does not love does not know God, for God is love."

Both words for love in this scripture are agape. Therefore, we know that if we do not know the one and only true God, we do not know this sacrificial, holy love that comes through the submission to His authority. That would leave us with only the romantic, sexual versions of love, and brotherly love, which were only created from the original definition of agape love, thus they are subjective. If we only have these two other versions, we will exalt emotions and invert the purpose of mankind, and our own fate. This is because we were created out of this agape love. Living in the New Age version of love which completely misses the true love of God is living a lie and a perversion of our own nature. As a result, love in New Age practices must constantly be fabricated and forced through chants/mantras, affirmations, and meditation practices.

With Jesus Christ, we abide in His love, we do not have to work to create our own love. With Jesus Christ, we no longer have to work to become like God either, nor to make a name for ourselves, nor to ascend through hidden knowledge that is promised through the New Age but never truly fulfilled.

And this is truly the greatest freedom and free gift ever offered to us.

ABOUT THE AUTHORS

Joscelyn Báez is a musician, professional dancer, writer, and business owner from Columbus, Ohio, who is passionate about exposing the darkness of the New Age spirituality movement and the Hollywood industry. She is the director of the upcoming short dance film "Mary Magdalene" that conveys her supernatural experience converting to Christianity when she lived in Los Angeles and fell into occultic practices.

Saba Tekle is a Publisher, Mentor, Entrepreneur Contributor, and Best-Selling Author. As the founder of 7 House Media, Saba has worked with over 200 authors worldwide. Saba has been featured in the Huffington Post, Entrepreneur, and Essence.

References

Energy and Awakening: A Psycho-Sexual Interpretation of Kundalini Awakening Steve Taylor, Ph.D. Leeds, United Kingdom

Near-Death Experiences and Kundalini Awakening: Exploring the Link Yvonne Kason, M.D., C.C.F.P., M.Ed., F.C.F.P. University of Toronto

* https://www.britannica.com/topic/New-Age-movement
* https://www.olivetree.com/blog/5-greek-hebrew-words-love/
* https://wiki.geneseo.edu/display/gender/Group+1%3A+
+Men%2C+masculinities%2C+and+sexualities+across+time+and+space
* https://www.compellingtruth.org/asherah.html
* http://kukis.org/Doctrines/Ashtoreth.pdf
* https://www.bibletools.org/index.cfm/fuseaction/Topical.show/RTD/cgg/ID/4962/Men-Renown.htm
* https://dbpedia.org/page/Babalon
* *Buddhism - World History Encyclopedia.* https://www.worldhistory.org/buddhism/
* *Cultural Atlas.* https://culturalatlas.sbs.com.au/religions/buddhism-mahayana/resources/buddhism-mahayana-rituals-and-practices

Alice Bailey 10 Point Plan to Destroy Christianity - Inspired Walk. https://www.inspiredwalk.com/6297/alice-baileys-10-point-plan-to-destroy-christianity

*https://www.lucistrust.org/arcane_school/talks_and_articles/the_esoteric_meaning_lucifer

The Temple, Antichrist and the New World Order, Understanding Prophetic ... By Dr. Alan Pateman

www.ingramcontent.com/pod-product-compliance
Lightning Source LLC
Chambersburg PA
CBHW060332170426
42811CB00131BA/2430/J